Connie Williams

This Life: Through Grace, Hope Mercy

An inspirational testimony of miraculous and unbelievable favor

CONNIE WILLIAMS

The author of
Emily's Blues
Green
Jon and Lale's Dance
Confession of the Onion Ring King

To Dr. B.
From:
Connie Williams
2020

Connie Williams This Life: Through Grace Hope and Mercy

Copyright © 2017 by Connie Williams TX u -093-560
Library of Congress-in-Publication Data 08-03-17
All rights reserved. Written permission must be secured from the author/publisher to use or reproduce any part of this book, except for the Biblical references from the various Bibles and critical reviews or articles.

ISBN: 978-0-578-60150-2

Scripture quotations noted are from: The Holy Bibles

Cover design by C-Mae 2019

Cover Photo by Robbie Massey

A Williams Acorn Publication *AWAP*

Published in the United States of America

Dedication

This book is dedicated to my loving family and friends, especially to those who are in heaven with our Father.

My mother Lillie said:

It's a poor frog

That won't praise

His

Own

Pond

My father Jones said:

Things will come and go

As they will.

Connie Williams   This Life: Through
                              Grace Hope and Mercy

Contents 4
Acknowledgments 5
Introduction 10

Chapter 1   San Fernando Valley- Rage -Salvation   14

Chapter 2   Los Angeles – Blessings   21

Chapter 3   My Saving Grace in North Carolina   37

Chapter 4   After New Jersey - Broken Wings can be Healed   46

Chapter 5   Los Angeles - God – the highest Judge   53

Chapter 6   Hollywood miracle   65

Chapter 7   405 San Diego Freeway angels   87

Chapter 8   More Rage in the Valley   90

Chapter 9   A Child shall Lead   97

Chapter 10   God turns it around   106

Chapter 11   North Carolina – Rescue   120

Chapter 12   God will put me where He wants me to be   126

Chapter 13   Sausalito - Headlands -Some only dream about   147

Chapter 14   Give God praise for Contracts   187

Chapter 15   Only God can create a Prince   195

Chapter 16   It's me; it's me, O Lord   205

Chapter 17   What God led me to Know   223

Chapter 18   I must stay on the Course   255

Chapter 19   Answer His callings   271

Notes 285
Family Photos 287
Sources 289
Other books by the author 292
About the Author 298

Acknowledgments

First giving thanks and honor to God for his favor and miracles—events that appear to be contrary to the laws of nature, the laws of a man ordered society, making sure we don't descend into chaos; **the laws of nature** revealed in ordered patterns. However, I'm referring to occurrences regarded as acts that only God can cause to happen-- events or actions that are amazing, extraordinary, or unexpected and unexplainable having taken place over the course of my life.

>And call upon me in the day of trouble:
>I will deliver thee, and thou shalt glorify
>Me. (Psalm 50:15).

Next there are some I must thank: Mama and Daddy: my parents, the late Jones McConnie Williams and the late Lillie Mae Williams for bringing me into this world. They were God-fearing believers and hard-working parents who raised eleven children, all who turned out well, from becoming college graduates to successful citizens in the business sector in a time when society and people have unfortunately become harsher and more uncaring in this world.

It's such a long path from poverty to professionalism—transcending from thirteen people, eleven youths and two adults, living in a two bedroom house in Monroe, NC, on Fairley Avenue to a high school English instructor and college professor of English Composition; Rhetoric and Inquiry at the University of North Carolina at Charlotte. God does create miracles!

My father took great pride in an educated mind—after serving in the Army's officers' training program and fighting in the Philippians during WWII; he matriculated at Shaw University in Raleigh, NC. His children could not escape emulating those thought processes and want to hold true to the ideas he cherished and exemplified. It is because of him and especially Mom, both were story tellers, that I am able to share these inspirational life experiences. This book is a testimony of God's extraordinary miracles in my life.

I must thank my Pastor. In a meeting with one of our Missionary Ministry leaders, Martha Hall and the Reverend, Doctor Leonzo D. Lynch of Ebenezer Baptist Church, Charlotte, NC, I once showed him the unfinished galley for this book, *This Life: Through Grace Hope and Mercy*. He had a look at the rough galley and then asked me "How long will it take you to write this one?"

I answered him by saying, "But I'm working on *Green*." (I was referring to another work in progress, entitled *Green*, that I began writing while a Writing Fellow at Headlands Center for the Arts in Sausalito, CA).

He responded, **"I didn't ask you that. I asked you, how long will it take you to write this one."** He pointed to the galley of TL: TGHAM again, that I had lain on the table in front of him.

I answered him, "I believe it may take about two years."

He responded, "Write this one next." He pointed to the galley again.

Although I went on to write my second book, *Green* first, because God laid it on my heart, and then I went on to write my parents' story, *Jon and Lale's Dance*. The Reverend's words have resonated in my memory until now, as I actually write the one, he suggested. Thank you for your inspiration Reverend Lynch.

A huge thank you is extended to all those who have supported this process: My loving family: beautiful children, grandchildren, siblings, a host of nieces and nephews; cousins and their friends who have tolerated me each time I began talking about my writing. They simply say, "We're so proud of you!" Bless their hearts.

Thanks to my church family members and other organizations: Ebenezer Baptist, Antioch Baptist; Blessed Assurance; Mount Olive African Methodist; and friends at Mount Carmel. And more recently, the ministers, congregation and business associates I met at the Church of God In Christ (COGIC) AIM Convention 2017 at the Charlotte, NC Convention Center, who prayed over my writing success; the Winchester Alumni Association; the Winchester Class Reunion of 62 they've presented and supported these works all the way without hesitation. And especially to the Event Planning Team, Audrey Wallace, and Nadine Henry, of Affairs to Remember; Dot Siler and Ms. Gwyn at the McCrorey YMCA; Ms. C-Johnson at Hickory Grove Library and Sandy Seawright, who housed my first edition of *Emily's Blues* at Barnes and Noble in the late eighty's; he was also influential in introducing my titles to Ms. Vickie Chapman at West Boulevard Library; Maurice Trull at McEwen Funeral Service in Monroe—a lifetime family acquaintance; the illustrious Monroe Sherriff Mr. F. McGurit, Surluta Belton of Monroe Local Government, The Williams and the Horton/Blackmon Family Reunions; Cory McManus Senior Attorney McManus Law Firm; UNC, Charlotte Literary Festival; The Chessington Homeowners Association; Brothers Foreign Cars; Dr. Phillippi and Crystal; J. McDonald, Attorney at Law; High Top Construction; Hendricks Motors; Folgers Car Dealership; Havertys Furniture; Ashley Furniture; Barbara Ann and nurses at Firsts Charlotte Physicians; The Massey family; Maria Macon, Myrtle and Pastor Moore; The Funderburkes; colleagues from the Big "G" high school: Viola Roseboro, Latarsha Roberts, Mariah King, Rachael Lloyd all says they can't wait to read it! Brenda Slade, Liz Williams, Jo Ella Ferrell; Jo Ann Smith, of course, Linda Hairston-always there with a smile, a chuckle, a willing spirit to edit; The McAuley's', The Barretts, The Carlocks; Dr. Liesman, Pediatrist; Johnson C. Smith University; Leonard and Christine, Shelia Dickens; Dori Sanders Farm; Robin and William Brown, all of whom have made a conscious effort to involve my works and or encourage this process whenever and wherever they can.

Over the years, thanks Robbie, my God-sent mate who shares my religious beliefs and gives his unconditional steady support.

Thanks also to three more men who miraculously influenced my life in unforgettable ways that I will share among other events in this book: First, the late Mr. Robert Moore of Bob More Photography in Hollywood, CA, whom I considered him my California father. Bob's endeavor was to assist in my eventually landing a part in a movie, so he set out to include me in the Hollywood social settings, and introduce me to movie stars, producers, agencies and the like. Through his effort I became the cover girl of Jive Magazine.

Next is the late Dr. George Herrick, English Emeritus, of Los Angeles Van Nuys Junior College who saw to it that I was an integral part of that college life. I believe because I was among the top third in his English class, especially when I made 'A's on his Literature Analysis tests, he became adamant about the manifestation of my first book that he edited, *Emily's Blues*.

And the last of these, but certainly not least, is the late Mr. Alex Haley, author of *Roots* and *The Autobiography of Malcolm X*, who cared enough to tell me the welcomed but "hard-core truth" about becoming a writer.

Introduction

∞

Once I lost a pearl, diamond and gold ring. I searched every known hole and behind every door in the house finally giving up from exhaustion and not finding that thing that once gave me pleasure to see it on my pointer finger, feeling it lost to the unknown forever and not to be found.

But God knew; He knew where and when to reveal the lost pearl and diamond gold ring to me again.

It wasn't in a week, or a month, or even a year. I believe He wanted me to give in to the unknown, surrender understanding that we lose some things and acceptance is growth.

Then one day a single look down there by the closet door, there at the bottom of a knitted and

Connie Williams   This Life: Through
                                      Grace Hope and Mercy

woven shoulder bag hanging there for some time, was a sparkle that caught my eye.

There in the bottom of the shoulder bag, I was shown the pearl, diamond and gold ring that God had preserved over the time that I didn't know where it was.

I took my hand and reached down inside and picked it up—rejoicing as I placed it on my pointed finger while simultaneously giving Him the honor and praise for continuing to make miracles in my life every day. For He is Honor, for He is Glorious, for He is Lord!

I **have always known** a thing of beauty even in my youth. At age seven I observed the huge mysteriously warm yellow ball flickering through the wooded pine trees across the street where I ran to in the summertime when we lived on the Old Charlotte Road in the early 50s in North Carolina; where I cleared a space on the ground, played house; pretended to boiled leaves in an empty pork-n-bean can on a make-believe stove preparing dinner for Cisco Kid, my imaginary family, before being called in by Mama at dust.

At night I looked outside the window; I talked to God and the man in the moon. "I see the moon and the moon sees me. God bless the moon and God bless me."

At that same age, I observed the whitest little balls falling magically from the sky from heaven to the ground when I snuck outside to scoop the icy substance into a bowl, later added Pet milk, sugar and

Connie Williams   This Life: Through Grace Hope and Mercy

Vanilla flavoring to make snow cream that oozed down our throats and made my siblings and me happy.

Later at age nine, where we lived on Fairley Avenue, a little silver spoon was shipped to me in the mailbox once I saved up two shiny dimes (twenty-cents), taped them with Scotch tape to the bottom of a letter when I applied to the Sweetheart Soap Company and later received the spoon in a box in the mail from New York with my name on the label. And I equated it all to the wonders of God the maker of all that is good and miraculous.

The Lord is my Shepherd I shall not want: (Psalm 23rd).

Hello God, it's me,

I use to wonder why I was given children to raise at a time when I was only a baby myself; born during the age of the Baby Boomers and Jim Crow; in North Carolina—four babies by the age of nineteen.

God I often pondered how I was expected to survive in this world of cruel people, myself being only five feet two in high heels and married off at age fifteen to a man who disrespected me, who wasn't even my baby's father, who was an abusive alcoholic that I nor my parents knew, and we began living in a roach infested house in North Carolina in the early 60s.

I was often saddened and questioned how I was expected to survive this cruel life, being dragged around from place to place, first individually and later with my young children, living in my home state, then later in New York, New Jersey, Washington, DC, and finally in California away from any family protection, without an education with one infant in my arms and another fetus in my abdomen, sometimes hungry, tired and afraid—afraid of the abusive mate and afraid to return to NC to live deprived in the poverty I knew there.

Connie Williams   This Life: Through Grace Hope and Mercy

I am reminded now of the long journeys in my life from day to day to reach this Point in Time: The journeys through half deserted streets, dangerous landscapes, holding unfriendly elements in all those places. *AND I NOW BELIEVE* God continuously spared my life numerous times from detrimental experiences so that I could glorify Him in the telling of how he delivered me in times of trouble. *HAVE MERCY UPON ME*, O God, according to thy loving-kindness: according unto the multitude of thy tender mercies blot out my transgressions. (Psalm 51:1).

Chapter 1

∞

*S*o there I **was** in the San Fernando Valley, California at the tender age of twenty-two, before development of the frontal lobe when one has the ability to decipher the consequences for choices; I was raising four children; away from any family support—not mother, father, sister, brother nor cousin to turn to and bear my soul when in need of comfort and encouragement, perhaps some words of wisdom. I had been wronged—I felt. Someone I had befriended, who was, I believed proving himself to be comforting; Jon had borrowed money from me which I needed—expected to be repaid. Knowing this, I was simply requesting to receive the change owed to me.

Jon and I had been neighbors living in the 54th Street community in Los Angeles and met sometime before moving to the San Fernando Valley. This "friend" Jon, who borrowed the money stood there on the sidewalk of Osborne and Glen Oaks Boulevard in the Valley speaking indignant and disrespectful, evoking feelings and the horrible and negative memories of years I had suffered abuse, pain; the treatment of being treated less than a child of God to be loved and honored. To say the very least, I was hurt, and I felt ashamed when he uttered words that I never expected to come from the mouth of my friend, when I asked for the money.

Jon's responded to me, "So what, you can't do anything about it."

I was sure he meant I was no threat to the six foot four man; therefore, I could not take what was rightfully mine. Again, I was a little girl in the big city with nothing, no one, and no support system.

Right before this time, I had been a night student at one of the local schools in Compton, CA, where the X husband had moved us to be close to his job, before my moved to the Valley. Compton represented a painful memory of Walter's violence toward me when I asked him one day for a separation and he tried to strangle me on the kitchen floor with his hands. (Which is a long story in itself, and told in the autobiography entitled, *Emily's Blues*). **Compton** is a city in southern Los Angeles County, California, United States, [11] situated south of downtown Los

Angeles. Compton is one of the oldest cities in the county and on May 11, 1888, was the eighth city to incorporate.

At Compton High night school, I sometimes was afraid of the outside riffraff, those young men hanging around the campus with less than honorable intentions—desires other than getting an education, who approached me to make passes, like, "Hey Baby can I get your number; can I go home with you; or can I take you home with me?"

I talked to the local authorities, the police, about my fears. I was simply told, "If someone tries to bother you, just run over them." Well my logical thinking told me first I would need to make it to and get inside my car. Then I would have to crank up and pull off. A lot can happen while trying to manage to drive off under such a threatening situation.

So, I took it upon myself to purchase and register a twenty-two-caliber pistol for my own safety and protection. Of course, I did not desire to shoot anyone unless I was in grave danger for my life. But I did imagine that the sight of the weapon would deter some unwanted aggression.

Consequently, when the money owed wasn't readily offered, I instantly felt snubbed; I felt my blood boil. Intending to avenge a wrong done to me, I took that twenty-two-caliber pistol and pointed at the culprit, Jon, with an endeavor to scare him into giving back the money that was rightfully mine.

The poor fool had the audacity to ask. "Oh, I guess you gone shoot me!?"

I said nothing as I stood there trembling with the gun pointed in his direction. I thought, of course I'm not going to shoot you!

"Then shoot if you think you're that bad!" Jon demanded.

I stood there momentarily in disbelief.

Then again calling my bluff, he uttered, "SHOOT!"
I thought--asked myself, IS THIS FOOL CRAZY?!
Totally caught up in the moment, I cocked the trigger, pointed directly at the culprit, aimed the gun and fired once, twice, then again for a third time back to back, Pow! Pow! Pow! My mind had certainly left me! If insanity had a name that night, it would have been mine. I was totally blinded to the fact that it was a friend, Jon standing there. But I didn't see **him**.
Each time I fired, "POW!" The first time God sent GRACE to grab that gun-- to redirect that bullet, instead of going through the gun barrel, the bullet astonishingly popped out of the top of the gun and fell onto the ground.
Jon stood there ducking and grabbing parts of his body that might have been hit.

The second time I fired, "POW!" God sent HOPE to take pity upon me and redirect that bullet.

And it too amazingly popped out of the top of that gun. It landed onto the ground in front of me because He couldn't allow His children to be destroyed.

Jon ducked again. I suppose he did not turn and run because he too was under the spell of disbelief.

The third time I fired, "POW!" God sent MERCY to forgive me, and the bullet remarkably popped out of the top of the gun landing onto the ground again landing in front of me.

In shock and blinded by rage, I turned and ran away, a short distance to my automobile like one running in a fog. I jumped into the car closed the door and drove away. By the time I drove the short distance to home from the corner of Glen Oaks Boulevard to Vaughn Street I was still under a blind spell. I didn't know at the time, what God had done for me. Foolishly, I cocked the gun once again, this time I fired into the ground. Seeing that the gun was now functioning properly, I climbed back into my Volkswagen, cranked it, but before I could drive off, the poor fool that I had attempted to shoot (kill), Jon opened the car door, flung the money into the car and closed the door and quickly walked away.

I turned off the car engine, climbed out and went inside the house. I sat down on the sofa and as if in a dream for a short distance in time I was motionless— my mind was blank. Jon showed up at the house only minutes later. He seemed to want to know if I was all right. The shame I experienced from my actions was overwhelming to my mind because I knew inside that my parents had raised me better than that. Then I thought of the shame I could have brought on my family by killing someone, especially those who figured that by my being in California by myself, I must be out here doing "God only knows what" wild and crazy stuff shown on the TV about Hollywood and the like. One of the Ten Commandments, "Thou shall not kill" flashed through my mind. Gladly, the moral compass of my upbringing kicked in as an aftermath—an inner sense which distinguishes what is right from what is wrong, functioning as a guide for morally appropriate behavior.

I asked Jon, "What are you doing here. I almost killed you tonight."

He showed the God inside of him—he had to be a God-fearing person because he instantly forgave me by revealing kindness just by being there with me. And afterwards he never once brought up the incident that could have become a tragedy for both of us.

Although what Jon did was wrong for not returning the money and being confrontational, what I realize today is that I wasn't attempting to kill him. I was trying to kill those harmful experiences that began at my childhood, at age fifteen and didn't end until I was twenty-two years old—abuse, disrespect; pain and despair I had suffered alone and all the days and nights of hardships—total displacement of aggression done to me by an X-husband , that he, Jon, had absolutely nothing to do with.

Many days, months, years later, I constantly thank you Lord—He literally worked overtime that night by sending His angels Grace, Hope, and Mercy to save my life. And I thank God as well for the person whose life I was inadvertently aiming to take because of a hand full of change. It was God's Grace, His Hope and His Mercy that kept me from losing my children and my freedom for the rest of my life. When I get ready to lash out at folk—Assignment: Tell the world who this is.

"I know that **my Redeemer** liveth."
(Job: 19:25)

In one of my favorite sermons preached by Reverend Bowers at Ebenezer Baptist Church (2017), in Charlotte, North Carolina recently, he said, "Tell your story; tell how God has blessed you— "Tell about God and drop the microphone."

****

Chapter 2

∞

*T*his I have come to know. God brings people in your life at the right place and at the right time. My instructor, Mr. Harrison Whitney became influential later in my fight for an education.

I've been fortunate to live in some states across America for a period in time long enough to understand and even become adapted to some of the cultural ways of living in a day to day learning process. I've breathed the crisp clean air of Canada when once we were searched and received clearance by the border patrol to crossed over; and I've seen the Canadian Rockies along the Continental Divide (It lies

along the main ranges of the **Rocky** Mountains), where my church group and I shopped for trinket souvenirs in the 80s. I've been to Mexico where the left side steering wheels and overcrowded streets led to vendors selling their wares and providing quick car maintenance; and I have ridden in a Mercedes taxicab along the streets in Nassau, Bahamas to restaurants that served fish with the head and eyes in tack along the white sand on the ocean, and swam in the Bahamas Western Atlantic Ocean with the little White Margate fish. I hope to get to Paris, France someday if God is willing, where James Baldwin (one of my idols) settled in Saint-Paul-de-Vence in the south of France in 1970.

Following the incidents at Compton High night school, I've attended schools and universities: Manual Arts High School in Los Angeles; Los Angeles Trade Tech College Founded in 1925 as the Frank Wiggins Trade School, Trade-Tech is the oldest of the nine public two-year colleges; Los Angeles Van Nuys College, (**Los Angeles Valley College)** is a community college located in the Valley Glen district of Los Angeles, California in the east-central San Fernando Valley, where God allowed me to earn an Associates of Arts Degree. While on a student fieldtrip, I've seen the San Andreas Fault. The San Andreas Fault is the most famous fault in the world. Its notoriety comes partly from the disastrous 1906 San Francisco earthquake, but rather more importantly because it passes through California.

While earning my Associates Degree, under the guidance and instruction of Dr. Harrison Whitney, who taught Afro American History at Los Angeles Van Nuys College, during the days of the Huey Newton and Bobby Seale Black Panthers uprising, we followed the episodic events.

One year before I arrived in CA the first time, in 1966, the Black Panthers were formed and played a short but important part in the civil rights movement, and the Angela Davis controversy when it was said that she, Davis, was a member of the Communist Party. The UC Board of Regents, at the urging of then-Gov. Ronald Reagan, tried to fire her before she even taught her first class at UCLA.

Later when I became a student on the college campus at Los Angeles Van Nuys Junior College, our instructor, Mr. Harrison Whitney kept us, his students informed of these current events. He connected the events of African history of the past to the current issues of history and life related to the present conditions for our people. He taught with such enthusiasm that he made me love teaching and I wanted to emulate his example.

Photo by Anthony Riley, Lake View Terrace, CA

During the Angela Davis controversy when she was prevented to teach, later enraged UCLA faculty, staff and students protested in support of Davis, citing academic freedom. A lawsuit also was later filed in Davis' defense.

Davis was allowed to teach a course that, for the opening lecture, had to be moved from the Dickson Art Center to Royce Hall

During those days in California as a student at Los Angeles Van Nuys College and later a student at Cal State University, Northridge, almost every woman of color wanted to identify with Angela Davis and what she represented —The ideology that "Black is Beautiful". So, like her, many wore the afro hairdo including me.

to accommodate more than 2,000 students and others who wanted to attend. A request for television cameras to broadcast the lecture was denied, but the controversy still made the national evening news. She taught that course as well as two others at UCLA during the 1969-70 academic years.

At the time of the Angela Davis episode, as a student at Los Angeles Van Nuys, a single twenty-two years old divorcee and mother of four children, I was receiving AFDC (Aid For Dependent Children). It was at this time that I developed the courage to ask the lady behind the desk at the Welfare office, "Can I use the funds to go to school and become a teacher?"

She pulled her eyeglasses down around her nose; looked up at me and stated, "That's absolutely unreal!"

I felt foolish for having asked such a question.

Aid to Families with Dependent Children was established by the Social Security Act of 1935 as a grant program to enable states to provide cash welfare payments for needy children who had been deprived of parental support or care because their father or mother was absent from the home, incapacitated, deceased, or unemployed. All 50 states, the District of Columbia, Guam, Puerto Rico, and the Virgin Islands operated an AFDC program. States defined "need," set their own benefit levels, established (within federal limitations) income and resource limits, and administered the program or supervised its administration. States were entitled to unlimited federal funds for reimbursement of benefit payments, at "matching" rates that were inversely related to state per capita income. States were required to provide aid to all persons who were in classes eligible under federal law and whose income and resources were within state-set limits. The Welfare tried to take away these funds because I was a full-time college student carrying twelve units instead of going to work full time, which the agency knew I could in no way earn enough wages to support four children.

Ms. Angela Davis' struggle and fight paralleled my own, her right to teach; I had to fight for my right to an education.

God gave me the wisdom to research the philosophy of the Welfare Department. I therefore submitted a long letter which stated: "The Welfare Department claims that they are for family Betterment. But in fact, it seems, according to what they are trying to do to me by forcing me out of college and an opportunity to a four-year college degree, that what their aim is, is to continue the cycle of welfare that many families are plagued with. I am trying to break that cycle of poverty by showing that to get a well-paying job; one must obtain a good education. This education will hopefully impact my children and other young mothers to follow in these same footsteps."

Additionally, it became necessary to solicit the help of my three Los Angeles Valley College Professors: Mr. H. Whitney; Ms. B. Stoffer; and Mr. G. Herrick to write letters to the Welfare Department attesting to my ability and need to complete my education with continued financial support to receive a four-year degree.

As fate would have it, God brought these Los Angeles Valley College instructors in my life at a time when I was struggling to raise my children and right at a time when I was about to lose the funding needed to continue to educate my mind.

Mr. Harrison Whitney's Letter of Recommendation

Los Angeles Valley College
58 Fulton Avenue
Van Nuys California 91401
President: Robert E. Horton

February 23, 1975

California State University, Northridge
18111 Nordhoff Street
Northridge, CA 91324

To Whom It May Concern:

This letter is to recommend Ms. Connie Sims for admission to California State University, at Northridge. As a student in my Afro IV and V classes, Ms. Sims has Proven herself to be a superior student in scholastic ability, dependability and scholastic achievement—as her over-all B+ average indicates.

Having known Ms. Sims for two years in the capacity as a student and as a member of a campus organization, I can testify that she is the mother of four (4) children and is solely responsible for their support.

I proudly recommend Ms. Sims for admission to CSUN and that she be given special consideration as an applicant for financial assistance.

Yours sincerely,
H. Whitney
Instructor

Connie Williams — This Life: Through Grace Hope and Mercy

Dr. Barbara Stoffer's Letter of Recommendation

Los Angeles Valley College January 20, 1975
58 Fulton Avenue
Van Nuys California 91401
President: Robert E. Horton

California State University, Northridge
18111 Nordhoff Street
Northridge, CA 91324

To Whom It May Concern:

Ms. Connie Sims, a student of mine, has told me some very disturbing news. She said that her education is to be disrupted by the welfare department. She further explained that since all of her children are school age, she will have to sign up for work and go out on interviews regularly.

I question this decision by welfare officials for several reasons. The purpose of this letter is for me to express my disapproval of what is happening to Ms. Sims.

First, she is an excellent student. She has an excellent academic mind that should not be wasted. With a college degree she could be an asset to the black community and the American society, instead of being a liability. Second, by graduation from a four-year institution she can serve as a model to her family and to other welfare recipients – you know….You can make it if you try….Third and last, Ms. Sims has a right to an education, and we, as taxpayers, have an obligation to help her in any way that we can. We cannot help her by pushing her out of school.

When, and if, Ms. Sims finds a job, her salary will probably be too meager to support herself and four teen-age daughters. The County will possibly have to subsidize her income. With a college degree, her income could foreseeably be high enough for her to pay income taxes, thereby enabling some other welfare recipient to get an education.

Moynihan, in his study of the black family, states that one generation of a family grows up on welfare and remains on welfare. Some of these families have been on welfare for as long as welfare has been in existence. Ms. Sims is trying to break this vicious cycle. She needs all of the encouragement that she can get. Let us do everything in our power to help her…not harm her.

Sincerely yours,

Barbara T. Stoffer
Instructor

Connie Williams   This Life: Through
                         Grace Hope and Mercy

Dr. George Herrick's Letter of Recommendation

5800 Fulton Avenue 91401   English Department
President: Robert E. Horton

Los Angeles Valley College   February 24, 1975
58 Fulton Avenue
Van Nuys California

Office of Admissions
California State University
Northridge, California

Dear Sirs:

It is a pleasure to recommend Ms. Connie Sims for favorable consideration for admission to California State University at Northridge. As a student in my English II class, Ms. Sims proved to be able, conscientious, diligent, and reliable. In brief, she was definitely a superior student. Further proof of her ability as a student is to be found in her over-all B+ average here at Valley College.

Ms. Sims has the very realistic goal of becoming an elementary school teacher, and as a member of the Parent Teacher Association, she has already done volunteer work at the Filmore School. Her rapport with and interest in children should aid her immeasurably in developing into an excellent teacher.

I know that Ms. Sims, despite the fact that she has four children, is receiving neither alimony from her former husband nor financial aid from her parents. Because of her dedication and capability, Ms. Sims should certainly be eligible for economic assistance at CSUN.

With no reservations whatsoever I strongly recommend that Ms. Sims be admitted to CSUN and that she be favorably considered as an applicant for financial help. As a student and later as an alumna, Ms. Sims should be a real credit to CSUN or to any academic institution that she attends.

Sincerely yours,

George H. Herrick
Associate Professor

By the Grace of God, my continued education was allowed and consequently not disrupted. These letters and my grade point average helped to put an end to the "disrupt your education and immediately get a job now" ideology.

Ironically, the Los Angeles Welfare Department came up with another strategy to disrupt my education-- get me out of school and away from completing my English Degree.

One of the upper-level personnel supervisors at the Los Angeles Department of the Welfare had been given the paperwork involving the decision to allow my continuation in school without any disruption of the AFDC funds. Shortly after I had won my case, this female individual called me at home one evening.

She commended me for carrying out the procedures "Fighting for my Rights" as she said, in such a professional manner. And she confessed that it was a first-time occurrence. According to her, "Usually, when there is a discrepancy between a Welfare client and the Department, it becomes extremely difficult to deal with. Most of the time the client is angry, and consequently they resort to using abrasive language to force their point. Sometimes it can even become violent."

She asked me, "Ms. Sims, how do you manage to keep such a "cool head" in matters like these?"

Of course, my answer was, "Anger won't help achieve anything." But mainly I thought, and then I confessed, "It takes God to fight these kinds of battles."

The lady chuckled, as if what I said was comical. Perhaps she chuckled because she was unfamiliar with our God.

The purpose for her call, she wanted to offer me a Welfare Spokesperson position, in her words and I quote: "You would make a great one to represent the Welfare mothers and speak to them about Welfare Services." She went on to say, "I admire how you have handled yourself when talking to me and the others here. You did not get upset nor yell. You were calm and organized and made everything clear of your intentions."

I thanked her, but I graciously declined her offer.

Connie Williams   This Life: Through Grace Hope and Mercy

Through God's blessings I knew I was connected to his vine.

Los Angeles Valley College
58 Fulton Avenue
Van Nuys California 91401
President: Robert E. Horton

April 18, 1975

Ms. Connie Sims
12514 Filmore Street
Lake View Terrace, CA 91321

Dear Connie:

Each semester Los Angeles Valley College recognizes high academic achievement on the part of outstanding students by placing their names on the Dean's list. It is my pleasure to notify you that you qualified for the Dean's list for the Fall 1975 semester.

Only those students who earn a grade point average of 3.5 or above in twelve units for the preceding semester, or who have completed thirty or more units at Valley College with a cumulative grade point average of at least 3.5 are eligible for inclusion on the Dean's list.

Please accept my personal congratulations upon your academic achievement. I know that the faculty and members of the administrative staff of the college join me in words of commendation for your success.

Enclosed is an invitation to the semi-annual Dean's Tea. We hope you will be able to participate in this college event in recognition of those Los Angeles Valley College students who have achieved superior academic records.

Sincerely,

Jack Neblett
Dean of Instruction

JN:mv

TAE
Tau Alpha Epsilon
Los Angeles Valley College
5800 Fulton Ave.
Van Nuys, CA 91401
February 22, 1975

Fellow Student,

We congratulate you on your outstanding performance of last semester. Because of your excellent record, we would like to extend to you this invitation to join Tau Alpha Epsilon.

TAE is the honor society at Valley College. However, of equal importance is the fact that we are also a service organization. We provide tutoring service, sponsor and participate in school and community activities. At the end of the semester scholarships ae awarded through our fund raising drives.

We urge you to attend our first meeting which will cover in some detail the club's social and scholastic activities and the privileges of being a member. Those of you who would like to be counted, but will be unable to attend meetings for any reason, can contact us through a note in TAE's BOX IN CC 102. In any event, we will be looking forward to seeing you or hearing from you. Our first meeting will be in CC 206 on Tuesday March 11, at 11 A.M. to prepare for Club Day. Subsequent meetings will be held every other Thursday.

If you wish to join, simply stop by the Business Office, fill in and leave the bottom of this invitation. Membership dues are $3.00. An additional initiation fee of $1.00 is paid by those who are new to TAE.
You must also have a PAID Student Body I.D. Please come and meet some friends!

Sincerely,

Leesa Lombardo, President
Sherry Zelickson, Secretary

It was at Los Angeles Van Nuys College that I made the Dean's List and qualified with a 3.5 Grade Point Average and was invited to join TAE, Tau Alpha Epsilon Sorority. Raising four children did not allow for sorority time—my platter was already overloaded.

I also experienced the guidance while at Los Angeles Van Nuys College of the late Dr. George Herrick, Processor of English, Emeritus; Cal State University, Northridge and the BSU (Black Student Union influences of Dr. William Burwell); and some years later the University of North Carolina at Charlotte, Master's program and as a Writing Fellow. *And praise, God,* although I've never experienced direct and blatant racism: name calling or threats, direct mistreatment, however, I'm not naïve to the possibility that the Welfare experience and my having to fight for an education could have very well been a case of overtly unfair treatment because of my race. But it did not faze me. More than anything else it gave me another testimonial of my Faith in the Almighty God.

> The **Serenity Prayer: God, grant me the Serenity** to accept the things I cannot change: Courage **to change the things I can**: And

Wisdom to know the difference. Reinhold Niebuhr (1892–1971).

Although I came up in a period of time in the 40s, 50s, and 60s, in the South when the races were divided and separate, and I am reminded of, at a very young age experiencing poverty and deprivation, and having been exposed to fear and violent raids of the KKK in my hometown where my cousin Robert F. Williams was the president of the NAACP, in Monroe, North Carolina, still, I wouldn't trade these youthful life experiences in this country for any other, even at the possibility of possessing earthly treasures.

I realize that I am not the only God-fearing individual who experienced being brought up in poverty where rats and roaches dwelled. There are numerous famous, wealthy, politically powerful individuals who unfortunately experienced a similarly deprived background—the ramifications of the ugly experiences of slavery in our background in this country, but because of sheer determination, those experiences did not prevent great successes in life. However, this determination and these successes in life can sometimes get in the way of one's mission—carrying out God's purpose for our lives.

****

Chapter 3

∞

Before living in California, one wouldn't think that there are unsafe elements while living in a secure home in North Carolina in the 60s. But there are; I became a believer from a harrowing event. As a young wife and mother of two babies at age 16, I assumed that behind closed doors there is protection. I soon learned differently, and that people can be deceptive, dangerous and harmful.

One evening while standing in front of the mirror in the privacy and assumed safety of my husband's parents—their home where we lived in North Carolina, I stood there in my nightgown brushing my hair. My mind was focused on what I was engaged in at the time.

    While continuing to brush my hair, I heard a faint sound like a crack outside the window. I didn't think much of it, that perhaps it was some small animal outside the window like a cat or a dog walking beneath the window where there were some dried-out low to the ground hedges. So, I paused the brushing of my hair for a moment to listen to hear if there would be another sound—there wasn't. I resumed the brushing, and didn't think too much more about it.

    Only moments later my father-in-law, Mr. T. Sims, came in the house completely out of breath and reported that he had been in the process of entering the house when he saw a male standing outside beneath the window of the room where I had been standing. He had vigorously chased the person down Walkup Avenue, but that the 'voyeur' had managed to out run him and escaped. He had absolutely no idea who the person was, but he recognized that the person was a black male (who didn't appear to be a teenager) who was quick on his feet. For some reason it was decided that the police weren't called. And the necessary precautions were made to tighten the window dressings.

    Then, unbelievably, perhaps six months to a year later; approximately 5:00 am one morning, my husband Walter (before we became divorced) had gone to work and as I lay in the bed, I felt a draft of wind coming from the back door. Our bedroom was situated on the front of the house and also next to the kitchen. As I lay in bed, I distinctly heard a 'tip, tip, tip' sound from someone moving toward the door to our bedroom. I thought it was my husband Walter having forgotten something, and returning to get whatever he had forgotten. I lay there listening and waiting with anticipation of his entering the room.

At five in the morning figures are shadowy, and I could see that the person was a tall male. His hair stuck out at the door where he stood. Again, thinking it was my husband, I called out to him. "Walter, is that you?" I said. There was no answer. Then the male proceeded to enter the bedroom, and he stood at the end of my bed with something white in his left hand that I couldn't make out what it was.

I became extremely scared. I couldn't move nor scream. I managed to call out only once and softly, "Maa-ma."

Miraculously Mrs. Sims, my mother-in-law who was sleeping in the bedroom a hallway and three rooms away; she heard my timid cry. She came running out of her bedroom and into the kitchen while shouting, "Who are you and what are you doing in this house!"

The person managed to immediately turn and escape out of the kitchen door and out from the back porch screened door.

I was so afraid—actually scared stiff. I was still in bed unable to move when my sister-in-law and mother-in-law came to the room. They had to help me manage to finally get out of bed.

The police were called immediately, and several tall, husky, white, Monroe police officers arrived and combed the kitchen where the criminal had been standing who had left a mud print of his hand on the wall beside the door to my room. It appeared and it was felt that he obviously had been hiding in the bushes beside the house when Walter left for work that morning.

The policemen roamed the front and back yard; they searched the back porch and the bushes. They were obviously angered and shaken by the occurrence and vowed if they had an iota of an idea who this criminal was, they would arrest him immediately.

Unfortunately, DNA hadn't been discovered in the early 60s; and, therefore the handprint left on the wall by the suspect at the door wasn't any help.

For the weeks that followed I was unable and too afraid to stay in the house alone on Walkup Avenue during the day. I was young, my children were babies, my sister-in-law was in school and my mother-in-law was a school teacher and my father-in-law worked for the Monroe Mayor and Walter worked at the bakery. So, after the incident, out of fear that the criminal might return, and I would be in the house alone, I usually went to my parents' house on Fairley during the day. My mother was at home and not employed at the time. For some time, almost every African American male I saw, I suspected.

Until this day, I have no idea what the object was he held in his left hand the few seconds he stood at the foot of my bed. I believe it very well could have been fatal had it not been for Mrs. Sims. Unfortunately, the criminal has never been caught.

Even now when I attend the Class of 62's Reunion and the Winchester Avenue Alumni Association Reunion in my hometown, I seldom think of the horrifying experience, after all it has been so many years ago and besides, at a time of enjoyment, I didn't want to mentally pass through some of the negative experiences in the years of my life. I do not know if that individual is still alive or passed away.

My saving grace was my Lord and Savior Jesus Christ. The cry out in the a.m. to my mother-in-law certainly wasn't a loud scream because I couldn't—in fact it wasn't a scream at all. It was a weak and fearful little distressful call, "Maa-ma" that God floated down the hallway pass the oil heater and my sister-in-law's bedroom where my children also slept and under the door and into Mrs. Sims' ear and allowed her to hear me; and He allowed her to know that I was in danger. Glory is to God Almighty the King of King and Lord of Lords. But in my distress, I cried out to the LORD; yes, I prayed to my **God** for help. He **heard** me from His sanctuary; **my cry** to Him reached His ears. (Psalm 18:6).

****

Throughout the nine-year marriage to Walter, in between his putting a loaded gun to my head just because he could, and the Monroe policeman telling me "JUST KILL HIM, NOTHING WILL HAPPEN TO YOU," and his hanging out in the streets, he just couldn't keep a job. He would find one, lose it, and leave the state to find another one. This time he had to leave North Carolina because of some trouble he had gotten into with the police over what he claimed was: "DEFINDING MY HONOR." On this particular night he had beaten a white man who drove through the neighborhood who asked if he had seen a young girl in white shorts, in reference to me. The next morning the police showed up at his parents' home with questions about the incident. So, Walter stood a good chance of going to jail.

He left North Carolina to relocate in New York where his two half-sisters lived to find employment. And once he was employed, he soon sent for Raven and me. We took a bus and joined him in New York.

It wasn't long before he lost this job for engaging in a fist fight with a coworker (he claimed it was a case of discrimination, but no charges were filed), and he was fired. One of his half-sister's wasn't too fond of Walter at all and didn't bite her tongue in the least in making us aware of how she truly felt. Therefore, we couldn't stay in New York.

In the meanwhile, I wanted to leave Walter; consequently, I had been in touch with my parents back in North Carolina who told me about an uncle in New Jersey. Mom sent bus fare for the transition.

Walter insisted on coming along. So, we took the bus to New Jersey where my Uncle Bristol lived.

For a short while we lived with one of the two girlfriends Uncle had, while he resided with the other one.

It soon became necessary for me to walk across Ridgefield Park in Patterson, New Jersey in 1960, at night in the dark carrying my child of maybe eight or nine months, while trying to get to the protection of my uncle, and a safe place. At this time the "X" would have abused me, as he often did, after losing his temper simply because I had a mind and could think and rationalize and of course this frightened him—if I could think and rationalize, then perhaps I might try and get away from him. Hence, he **needed to keep me in my place**. After striking me, he had gone to the neighborhood bar where he frequented on a regular basis until the wee hours of the morning.

As it turned out, Walter showed up at Uncle Bristol's to take my baby and me both to a rented room he found in a house on Euclid Street, but I refused to go. So, he stayed at my uncle's too, until my uncle insisted that he should go home. I was carrying another baby, and by then I must have been eight months. Later that week, I did return to the room upon Walter's demand that I go with him—so I did. Although I was eight months pregnant, I got down on my knees and filled the bathtub with water to scrub all of the dirty clothes to prepare to return to Monroe so that I could give birth to my new baby.

When I did return to Monroe, Walter soon quit his job with the Patterson Sanitation Department (where by the way, he made good money); he soon followed me approximately three weeks later back to North Carolina.

It's a wonder that I did not lose the baby or suffer a concussion or something far worse, from the blows inflicted about my head and face, but God took care of the babies and me.

> And he went a little farther, and
> fell on his face, and prayed, saying,
> O my Father, if it be possible, let this
> cup pass from me: nevertheless
> not as I will, but as thou wilt.
> (Matthew 26: 39)

He protected us from the dangers of walking across Ridgefield Park in a major city in the state of New Jersey and from the abusive alcoholic husband.

Once I returned to North Carolina, my second daughter, Pricilla was born weighting seven pounds; she was healthy and beautiful. God takes care of His babies.

I'm reminded of an old Christian song that my grandmother on my mother's side, Mama Allen, use to hum while sitting on her front porch next door to us on Fairley Avenue and listening to the radio, entitled: "There Is No Secret What God Can Do." What He's done for others, He'll do for you. With arms wide open He'll pardon you. There is no secret what God can do."

Now many, many years later at the Williams' family reunion in New Jersey, in 2000, I cannot help but reminisce of those horrible life experiences I suffered during my youth in my marriage that I couldn't do anything about that God brought me/us- my children and me through.

Chapter 4

∞

After living in New Jersey and returning to North Carolina for the birth of my second child, we lived in Washington, DC. Little did I realize that my connection with Washington would reach back to the days at New Hampshire Avenue NW, at age seventeen, and at Georgetown University Hospital where my third daughter, Dawn was born. This connection resonates into my emotional experience in 2014 when lovely Michelle and President Obama after his election strolled down Pennsylvania Avenue in front of the White House , and where I use to hail down a taxi cab to catch a ride to the Old Post Office and mail letters to my mother and father back home in North Carolina.

My mind leads me back to an earlier time of my pregnancy with my third daughter one night before she was born, when I bolted out of the back door of the basement apartment we shared with the janitor of the building where we lived. Although it had snowed, I ran through the snow to try to keep from being hit. Her father Walter chased after me. He quickly caught up with me; he pulled me back inside striking me several times all about the head and face because of something insignificant I said that he did not like. Of course, I was out of breath when he caught up with me, and after he struck me of course I couldn't help but cry.

Believe it or not, Walter always seemed to believe he could smooth over every act of violence he inflicted upon me by pleading for my forgiveness.

"Baby, will you give me another chance." was always his line.

I had to forgive him. I was afraid not to—at age seventeen with two babies, and another child on the way, at the time, where else could I go?

When I think back to how horrific those experiences were, I must admit, it could have been worse. I absolutely know that God spared my life, and He did it for a specific reason.

Can these broken wings be healed?
Broken wings of disappointment….
(Isaiah 40:29) NLT
Faith in the midst of fear: Faith is
The substance of things hoped for and

The evidence of things not seen.
(Hebrew Chapter 11:1)

Then in 1986, the memory of my experiences in Washington, DC derived from even another perspective. While teaching at Piedmont High School, in Union County, as a teacher of English and Economics, Legal and Political Systems, under Social Studies, it was necessary to organize, raise funds to sponsors a number of students on a field trip to Washington, DC in the Close-Up High School Program, a one week's governmental studies program designed to give students and educators an inside look at their democracy in action. I've taken students on this action-packed trip three times. If one is to tour D.C. this is one-of-a-kind opportunity. Students and instructors are flown to DC and usually all housed with security and chaperones at **Crystal City** an urban neighborhood located in the southeastern corner of **Arlington** County, **Virginia**, south of downtown Washington, D.C

Before going on the trip, one special student worthy of mentioning from my Social Studies class, a very bright and straight- 'A'-polite young man was to attend. He was the highway patrolman's son. Although it was totally unnecessary (the funds poured in from doctors and lawyers to sponsor his fees), but Daniel wanted the experience of employment, so he took a job to supplement funds for his trip working at the local fish restaurant directly down on Sykes Mill Road, the street from the school and from where he lived.

On the way to work one afternoon, unfortunately, he and another student decided to car race down the street to the job location, only a short distance away. As it turned out, the "prince of a boy", Daniel lost control of his automobile, hitting a telephone pole guidewire, and poor Daniel instantly lost his precious life.

It was so difficult to understand why this lovely boy had to lose his life when trying to do something good. Our school, community and I were totally devastated. But there is one thing I do know with my entire mind. And that is God does not make mistakes. And there is one thing I truly do believe. Daniel was too good to remain here on earth. I believe that God had to take him at age sixteen and not leave it to chance and free will before the people of the world influenced him.

> **God** cannot **make mistakes**. If **God** is Perfect, meaning He has not sinned and never will sin; **God did not** make a mistake In creating mankind. (Genesis: 6)

****

Although our trip to DC definitely had its downside with the loss of a wonderful student, poor Daniel, yet a visit that was made still influences my life today. While in Washington, I toured Ana Costa, South East, and the home of one of my hero's Fredrick Douglass the self-taught run-away slave who made a profound impression upon my psyche with his speech: Oration, Delivered in Corinthian Hall, Rochester, July 5, 1852, to the Congress about July 4, Independence Day.

In Mr. Douglass's Ana Costa living room there were 'two' small size Mahogany writing desks. Back then, when I lived in a condo, I was so inspired by this arrangement of his writing space that I could hardly wait to return home to rearrange my living and dining area to create a writing space easily accessible for writing of my own to replicate what I had seen. I already had a temporary writing area in my bedroom, but now, I wanted to create a permanent one.

While on the Close-Up trip, I stood on the floor of the Rotunda; ate Caviar on salad at the Press Club (where President Obama had his luncheon). My experience was right before participating in the taping of Ron Glaser's TV show on CSPAN, "Television Point of View." Of course we visited the Lincoln Memorial; Washington Monument; House and Senate; and I rode the Yellow and Blue Line Transits; went to Foggy Bottom, the Arlington Cemetery; and the Henri Matisse art exhibit, the Bureau of Engraving and Printing; The Supreme Court; the Library of Congress where the clerk pulled up a printout of my very own book *Emily's Blues*, which was quite thrilling, among some other educational and cultural events.

Ironically, right across the street from Frederick Douglass's home was a homeless Black man sleeping under the bridge on the concrete in Washington, DC in 1986. I wondered if he was possibly a Vietnam military veteran that is so often forgotten once they become a civilian.

So today, as a tribute to Mr. Frederick Douglass, my hero, now that I have transitioned into a larger home, my writing space is now located in my great room with a Mahogany Van Buren Writing Desk that I proudly invested in, 2015. (I was finally able to disassemble the kitchen table used as a dining room table that I was using as a writing desk, that was entirely too high and too uncomfortable to write on without creating a strain on the arms and my neck; I literally don't know how I managed to write a book on that kitchen table). The Van Buren situated in the great room is surrounded by a large print Bible given to me from my baby daughter, the late Camille-God rest her soul and husband Al, also a small stack of best-seller author's books, including *Beach Music*, and a stack of best seller books stacked against the hall wall that leads from the living room. My computer and printer, two lamps—one to the left of me and the other to the right, two small tables, all representing my "Ivory Tower" my writing space where I go to conduct research and create. As one visitor said when he saw the writing space, "Oh, so this is where it goes down!"

I'm reminded of Mark Nepo on Oprah who talked about "soul" the inner core that houses the spirit. He said, "Excellence is fine, but I write to connect with every other writer that has written to express the flow of thought and energy to reach a listening spirit to receive the beauty of creation." His words reach into my mind, my heart and my gut. To add to his words, I write to get the story told.

All the times God spared my life, it was because He wasn't through with me yet—I truly know it was for many reasons like this—my mission in life.

> God opens doors that cannot be
> Shut. (Philippians: 1:3-6) NVI.
> God started it he inaugurated it.

> For verily I say unto you, That whosoever shall say unto this mountain, Be thou removed, and be thou cast into the sea; and shall not doubt in his heart, but shall believe that those things which he saith shall come to pass; he shall have whatsoever he saith. Therefore, I say unto you, What things so ever ye desire, when ye pray, believe that ye receive them, and ye shall have them. (Mark 11: 23-24).

Chapter 5

∞

In the year 1967, I had taken the Southern Pacific train to California with my four children. We were joining Walter once again, this time in Los Angeles. And one year later in 1968 the same year everyone was mourning the assassination of Dr. Martin Luther King, our marriage fell apart. The father of my children, who also matriculated, believe it or not, in the academia, as a former Sociology major at Johnson C. Smith University, who should have been ashamed of himself, and who should have tried to demonstrate for our children what Martin Luther King stood for—equality for all Americans and self-pride, the pride his parents also tried to instill in him. Consequently, instead of holding the family up, there he was tearing it down. He was sentenced to Soledad Prison for two years for attempting to rob a Los Angeles bank during the middle of the day, directly down the street from where we lived.

Soledad is serviced by the Monterey-Salinas Transit line 23. Some weeks later, at the suggestion of his correctional officer, who accompanied me on the long ride to the prison, we took the Transit line to visited Walter. He sat behind bars with his lips squeezed tightly together and a malicious expression of intimidation. And when he spoke, he told me, "You know I'm going to kill you when I get out of here."

I believe I filed for a divorce the next week. I therefore divorced Walter while he was incarcerated. There was no other way to get him out of my life. Some parts of this story, I reveal for the benefit of those who haven't read *Emily's Blues*, my autobiography.

Anyway, so, there I was, thrown into a life alone as a single mother of four on the West Coast.

Following becoming a single mother without a formal education (I had already began attending Adult Night School at Manual Arts High); I did not have a job to provide for the support of my children. I was therefore entitled to government support.

With the government funds, I moved my children to a nicer place, a stucco duplex house on

54th Street and Vermont Avenue with a nicely well-kept backyard where the children could play. I was so happy that the owner, an African American female nurse, who worked at one of the local hospitals in the Los Angeles area, she accepted and approved my application to rent.

On the day I was to submit the deposit check to rent the duplex, I met both the woman and her extremely "cockeyed" husband who came with her to the duplex. He managed to focus one eye on me while the other eye aimed in another direction as he handed me the key.

The children and me in Los Angeles on 54th street at Easter. Taken by the children's Aunt Lizzie.

Shortly after completing the move in, nearly a week passed, when the owner's husband began coming over to the house to mow the lawn, weed the grass and sometimes he watered the grass in the early hours that the children were in school. He actually spent hours on this work. I could see him in the back yard with one eye on his work and the other eye it seemingly pointed in my window, in my direction.

I myself was in school two nights a week at Manual Adult Night School. My neighbors who lived directly next door had two children, two teenagers who attended the Catholic school up the street on 54th and Vermont agreed to watch my children on the nights I was in school.

So, during the day, while my children were in school, I was usually at home, cleaning, cooking and completing my homework for school.

One morning after the children had gone to school, I lay in bed, ironically turned over and discovered the cockeyed landlord standing in the doorway to my bedroom. He had taken his key and come into my home.

For a second or two I was scared stiff. I couldn't move; I didn't know which way to turn or what to say. A cold chill moved up my spine as I slowly pulled the covers up around my neck and held them there tightly. I didn't know how long he had been standing there, or what he had done while he was in my house.

"What are you doing here?" I managed to utter.

He stood there not responding seemingly lost in thought and time and aiming one of his eyes at me.

"Please leave." I begged him softly as I managed to get these words out.

Again, he did not respond, but turned and quickly exited the side door that he had entered.

I managed to collect myself, climb out of bed and scrambled to the door to lock it. I didn't know what would happen next since he had used his key to enter.

Shortly after he left, while I was dressing, the telephone rang. It was his wife calling me. She tried explaining, "My husband and I are very sorry about the mix up this morning. He had come over to check the water heater in the duplex. He had no idea you were at home."

I reminded her, "Neither one of you is to come into the place using a key. If you knock and no one answers, no one is to enter, not even to do repairs."

"I'm very sorry and it won't ever happen again." She pleaded.

Shortly after Walter was incarcerated and before moving into the duplex, I had befriended the neighbor Jon who lived next door to the apartment I moved from. This was also before the terrible event with the gun. As a friend, Jon assisted me in transportation to the grocery store. At the time, Walter nor I owned a car.

One afternoon when the landlord's husband was there again, mowing the grass, he told me, "I don't want that friend of yours coming in and out of my house using my water, wearing and tearing my house."

Then finally one evening after my children were in bed and asleep, (on school nights they went to bed routinely around nine), there was a knock at the door, I went to answer it, I could see there were policemen everywhere—on the front porch, on the side of the house, and in the back yard looking into my windows.

I opened the door and several tall, huge Euro American Los Angeles policemen flooded into my living room.

One officer told me, "The man who owns the house has complained that there is drug usage going on in this house."

Of course, there wasn't because as I told the officer, "The man is lying and I don't know why; I'm a mother of four children and a student at the local Manual Arts Adult night school. And I do not use any form of drugs, and I never have used drugs for any reason at any time."

The Policemen still searched the premises with my children in bed. As a young mother, naïve to the trickery of an envious man with obvious evil intensions; therefore, the thought of asking if they had a search warrant did not occur to me. They terrified me so profoundly, and I began to cry hysterically. After the search and they not finding any drugs, left without as much as the decency of an apology.

A day or two later the cockeyed landlord served an eviction notice to me to vacate the duplex. If my memory serves me correctly, the paperwork said: THIRTY DAYS TO VACATE THE PROPERTY. He didn't care that this would interrupt my children's lives and education by having to move and change schools.

I could not pay rent and accumulate the funds to relocate at the same time, so I discontinued paying any rent.

Fortunately, I located a new apartment owned by a beautiful and fashionable middle class young African American woman who wore a wide western fedora, and drove around Los Angeles in an orange Corvette, lived in her own home and slept in a huge round bed like Tina Turner in "What's Love Got to do With It?" Sometimes after meeting her, I often wondered what that life style was like. I observed from a distance; I never had a chance to ask her.

The apartment I rented was located farther west in the Los Angeles area too, and I managed to move before Thanksgiving. My brother Chet visited and had Thanksgiving dinner with my children, Jon and me on his way to serve in the military during the Vietnam crisis.

We were pretty settled into the new apartment, thanks to our Father in heaven with the children then attending the new Western Avenue Elementary School that was in walking distance. Reluctantly, Chet left us about one week later to report for duty with the Marine Corp.

Four days after April 4th, 1968 when Martin Luther King was assassinated, I was awakened on the morning of April 8th, 1968, 6:29 am PST to the rumbling of a thunderous shaking of the 1968 earthquake that moved the entire building from side to side. When the Borrego Mountain earthquake struck in 1968, it was the largest and most damaging quake to have hit southern California since the <u>Kern County earthquake,</u> 16 years earlier. It was felt as far away as Las Vegas, Fresno, and even Yosemite Valley. The quake caused damage across most of southern California -- power lines were severed in San Diego County, plaster cracked in Los Angeles, and the *Queen Mary*, in dry-dock at Long Beach, rocked back and forth on its keel blocks for 5 minutes. A few ceilings collapsed at various places in the Imperial Valley. Close to the epicenter, the quake caused landslides, hurling large boulders down slopes, damaging campers' vehicles at Anza-Borrego Desert State Park, and caused minor surface rupture, cracking Highway 78 at Ocotillo Wells. As it turned out my children all slept through the occurrence. *God is an awesome God.*

The earthquake caused damage to the apartment buildings in the area and we unfortunately had to move yet again. So, we moved to the San Fernando Valley into a house on Vaughn Street and my children were enrolled into Fillmore Street School. Welcome to the "**Valley** of the Stars," Southern California's **San Fernando Valley**, cities of Burbank, Calabasas, Glendale, **Los Angeles**, and San Fernando is approximately an hour and a half from downtown Los Angeles.

I had completed my course of study at Central City, a Division of Adult and Career Education in Los

Angeles. Thinking that the duplex matter and the cockeyed landlord episode was over, right when I thought I could breathe, relax and once again settle in, along came negativity: This is when I began getting papers from a prominent California lawyer because the owner of the Los Angeles duplex filed a lawsuit against me for unpaid rent.

In the meanwhile, the house on Vaughn Street needed repairs and the owner had begun to make them by tearing out the bedroom wall. So, we moved again, this time into a three-bedroom apartment, fortunately directly across the street from Fillmore Street School, my children's school and the beautiful neighborhood park.

The unresolved issue of payment of rent in Los Angeles was unfortunately still being pursued by the harebrained landlord, which resulted in the court system sending papers of a judgment against me for thousands of dollars in fines for payments in the arrears, and that I needed to appear in the Los Angeles Court.

On the morning I was to appear in court, Jon was kind enough to drive me into downtown Los Angeles during the hustle and bustle of the morning traffic, exhaust depositing fine automobiles, yellow RTDs that opened the doors to thousands of riders stepping off in route to work; skyscraper building poking the sky.

The Clara Shortridge Foltz Criminal Justice Center is the county **courthouse** in **downtown Los Angeles**, California, United States. It is located at 210 West Temple Street, between Broadway and Spring

Street. Originally known as the Criminal **Courts Building**, in 2002 it was renamed The Clara Shortridge Foltz Criminal Justice Center. The **building** houses the main offices of the **Los Angeles** County Public.

The courtroom was bulging with people of all shapes and colors from all walks of life. I had never before witnessed anything like it. And I was scared to death. I literally had no idea of what to expect. After all, I was there without representation. I could not afford a lawyer. I simply planned on pleading my case and asking for understanding.

After approximately an hour of being there, when the Euro-American gray-haired judge called my name and the case number, I stood and the roaming eyed landlord who was seated across the courtroom on the other side, he stood with one eye looking at the judge and the other one looking east.

The judge took one look at me, a petite five feet; one hundred-five pounds and looked at those two hundred seventy pounds, six feet three, African American squinting eyed man, he asked, "Where is your wife, the Mrs.?"

The tilted to one side eyed landlord answered, "She's not here your honor."

Then the judge questioned, "Isn't she the owner of the property?"

That cockeyed, harebrained, cockamamie landlord answered, "Yes she is the owner your honor. But she wasn't feeling well this morning."

The judge took time to scan over the courtroom and then at me and stated, "Mrs. Sims is here!" It seemed he emphasized with the distance I had travel from the Valley to downtown Los Angeles; I imagined that he understood the preparation it had taken, to plan for my children's care, and then to arrive on time at this unfamiliar place.

He took several moments to look over the paperwork in front of him; he hesitated another moment; then picked up his gavel to secure it with both of his hands. He held it in his right hand and quickly declared, "CASE DISMISSED!" and with one loud rap of the gavel down on the block striking surface, I was free—out of there. I wasted no time at all moving from the room-filled with spectators.

At the time, I thought I was in court without representation, but I am aware now that I was there with the COUNCIL THAT SITS ON HIGH, my Lord Jesus Christ. Only God could have performed such a miracle! Thank You Jesus!

> Gather my saints together unto me:
> those that have made a covenant with
> me by sacrifice. And the heavens shall
> declare him righteousness: for God is
> judge himself. (Psalm 50:5-6)

The God sent friend, Jon with the children and me.

This Photo was taken in the San Fernando Valley. The Photographer is unknown.

Chapter 6

∞

Hollywood was only a place I knew I passed on the way to my stenography classes at Los Angeles Trade Tech College in the morning from the San Fernando Valley, and I passed it in the afternoon from LA on the way home to Lakeview Terrace, until one day when I was leaving my gynecologist's office in Westwood. I stepped into an elevator and a well-dressed African American man carrying cameras with lots of large wires stepped onto the elevator and turned to speak to me.

"Have you ever done any modeling?" He asked.

I stood there in my hip-huggers and fitted lace above the waistline shirt and wedge-hill shoes; my hair that hung shoulder length and kept in place with a hairband placed around it. The thought flashed through my mind; *modeling is actually what I've always wanted to do all of my life*. And reality flashed through just as quickly before I had a chance to speak. "No, I haven't given it much thought." I answered cautiously, because he was a stranger, and we were alone in an elevator, although he didn't seem to be someone that might do me harm.

He introduced himself, "I'm Steve a photographer for the Sentinel Newspaper in Los Angeles, and I have a friend, a Hollywood photographer who might like to photograph you." He said as he stuck his hand into his pocket to pull out a business card. He offered it to me. "Here is his card. I think you should go and see him."

Although I accepted the card and thanked Steve, I didn't give going to Hollywood much thought at the time because I had such a full platter in the 70s—raising my four children as a single parent and my school studies. I was totally removed from the Hollywood world. Besides, I was apprehensive about getting involved with the Hollywood scene, especially with the wild movie stars stories in the media. The Black actor, Fred Williamson who starred in "The

Legend of Nigger Charlie" with D'UrVille Martin and the film "Black Caesar" was popular; the "Exorcist", "The Way We Were"; and "The Sting" were highly acclaimed movies of that time.

Of course I was aware of **William Horace Marshall** (August 19, 1924 – June 11, 2003) who was an American actor, director, and opera singer best known for his title role in the 1972 blaxploitation classic *Blacula* and its sequel *Scream Blacula Scream* (1973), as the "King of Cartoons" on the 1980s television show *Pee-wee's Playhouse* beginning with its second season, and an appearance as Dr. Richard Daystrom on the original *Star Trek* television series. He had a commanding height of 6 ft 5 in (1.96 m), as well as a deep bass voice. William Marshall lived down the street from us on Dronsfield that led to Hansen Dam Park in Lake View Terrace. On the way to the park, my children and I rode our ten-speeds right pass Mr. Marshall's house. He was well liked in the community and would invite neighborhood youths to swim in his pool on many occasions.

The area where we lived **Lake View Terrace** is a suburban district in the north east quadrant of the San Fernando Valley region of the City of Los Angeles, California.[1] **Hansen Dam** is a flood control dam in the northeastern San Fernando Valley, in the Lake View Terrace neighborhood of **Los Angeles**, **California**. The dam was built by the U.S. Army Corps of Engineers, Los Angeles District ... The **Hansen Dam** Recreation Center and **Park** are located there, with extensive day use facilities.

Surrounding areas include the Angeles National Forest, Little Tujunga Canyon, Big Tujunga Canyon, Hansen Dam, Kagel Canyon, and a portion of the Verdugo Mountains. The community lies adjacent to the communities of Sylmar, San Fernando, Shadow Hills, Sunland, Sun Valley, and Pacoima

The community is middle-class and ethnically mixed, including Latinos, African-Americans, Whites and Asians.

Eventually, one day during the summer when school was out, I became motivated to seek out the Hollywood photographer Robert Moore whose name was on the card.

I telephoned Mr. Moore.

Our conversation: "Steve from the LA Sentinel Newspaper gave me your card and said that I should call."

Following the telephone call and positive conversation with Bob Moore, I drove to Hollywood Blvd to his office and parked my Volkswagen on one of the side streets.

My impression of him and his office was inspiring. Photographs of African American Hollywood actors and models hung on all of his office walls: Actors like Leslie Uggams; Bill Withers; Jane Kennedy, Beverly Johnson, Leon Iassac, Kennedy, and many others.

He said, "Yes I would like to photograph you. I think you will make a pretty "cover girl" model.

He expressed his intention to photograph me for the cover of Jet Magazine. Eventually, I met with Bob on several occasions in his office. On one occasion, he took a photograph of me in a black bikini and black boots, taken near the train station somewhere that I don't exactly recall in Los Angeles. And another photo was taken in front of the Los Angeles Music Center wearing a purple "hot pants" and cape outfit also wearing a purple fedora that tied underneath my chin.

Over the next year or so, through Bob Moore I met Mr. Jackson of Jackson Motion Picture Company, who ironically was the brother of my Los Angeles medical doctor Dr. Jackson, MD.

Mr. Jackson of the motion picture company owned a Speakeasy night club in West Hollywood where I was invited to attend one evening. On the night I attended I invited my one and only girlfriend from Los Angeles, Wilma, whom I met at Manual Arts High School. Mr. Jackson stood at the door dressed all in white: white suit, shoes, shirt and tie. I remember he said as he opened the door and I entered, "This is one of my stars." I remember this particular night because inside the Speakeasy were the Temptations and the base singer's deep melodious voice could be heard over the crowd of Hollywood stars and attendees.

It is so ironic that today, Hollywood stars are coming out of the woodwork to tell their stories about sexual harassment from men in the movie industry that they experienced as far back as ten and twenty years ago. Even one of my movie idols Dustin Hoffman has now been accused of some unwanted sexual-related behavior, for which he has publicly apologized. And I therefore, feel compelled to tell how Mr. Jackson tried to "come on" to me. One evening while in his Hollywood Boulevard office, when he signed me as an extra in Charlton Heston's movie Soylent Green, I recall him alluding to some idea of taking me out on a date. And I turned him down. Mr. Jackson was old enough to be my father—like Bob Moore. Then I remember him telling me, "Baby you had better come on and get with me. There are a whole lot of women who want me."

And I remember thinking, "Then you need to go and get those so called "whole lot of women.'" Mr. Jackson agility was that of Fred Sanford. So being alone in his office didn't frighten me too much as long as I consciously kept a safe distance, besides, I felt if necessary, I could out run him.

I told Bob Moore about the incident soon after it happened.

Although Bob Moore and Mr. Jackson were business associates, I didn't actually know how far their friendship extended. But after I told Bob about the incident, it angered him; he vowed, while using some excessively stronger language, "I won't be introducing you to anymore, 'less than honorable producers' with questionable integrity."

A short time later, I met Jim Brown at the Candy Story another West Hollywood dance club with a female DJ (a tall, attractive, model type "fly girl") situated in the middle of the dance floor with huge stereo speakers and turntable that spun popular music of the 70s. That club was another regular hangout for many Black Hollywood stars such as Yaphet Kotto the star of "Live and Let Die" 1973. At the Candy Store, on the night I met Mr. Brown, with whom Bob had arranged a meeting because he was embarking upon the production of his new film "The Slams." D'UrVille Martin, star of "Five on the Black Hand Side" and a friend of Bob Moore introduced us. Jim Brown sat, with me situated in the middle, and D'UrVille Martin on the other side sat very close to each other on the bottom step of a stairway that led to the upper room of the Candy Store.

Sometime later at Disco 9000, another Hollywood night club, D'UrVille Martin told me how stunned he was when he saw me at the Candy Store with a new hairstyle. He told me, quite gentlemanly, "It was most attractive."

Bob Moore had expressed his determination to help me get a part in Jim Brown's new movie. He thought I would have done well portraying the girlfriend in the Gordon Parks movie, "Super Fly" staring Ron O'Neal, Max Julien and Richard Pryor.

Bob More was well known throughout the Hollywood scene. Some of his associates were Teddy Pendergrass, Bill Withers, who I met at the Essence Awards who was the host. At our table at the Essence Awards was Lee Craver a Hollywood agent who introduced me to Lionel Richie who was with the Commodores at the time. Of course Bob knew many of the "Big Wigs" in the magazine industry, Essence, Jet, Jive, Playboy and Penthouse, (I "once" attended a lunch with Bob at the Playboy Club in Hollywood— quite an awakening to see those Playgirl bunny waitresses) these were associates of his too because he photographed models for some of their books and magazines.

I also met Anthony Riley another Hollywood photographer and Mr. Moore's protégé, a student from Southwest College where Bob taught photography.

At this same time, in 1973 Charlton Heston was filming his Science Fiction movie "Soylent Green" with Leigh Taylor, Edward G. Robinson, Dick Van Patten, Chuck Connors and Paula Kelly. Through Jackson Motion Pictures, I became an extra in the movie that was set in future Manhattan and filmed at Metro-Golden-Mayer Studio in Culver City. In 2020 Earth is overpopulated and New York City has 40 million starving, poverty-stricken people. The only way they survive is with water rations and eating a mysterious food called Soylent. A detective investigates the murder of the president of the Soylent Company. The truth he uncovers is more disturbing than the Earth in turmoil when he learns the secret ingredient of Soylent Green.

In one of the street scenes where humans are being scooped up by a street cleaning truck to make food products, I stood there very close to and on the right side of Mr. Heston in the action scene where he was shot for protesting. This movie was Edward G. Robinson's last film.

Metro-Golden-Meyer Studios, the greatest **studio** in the history of Hollywood was never really in Hollywood. They were actually located in humble Culver City, some seven miles southwest of Hollywood & Vine, closer to Marina Del Rey than to Hollywood. M-G-M was the most powerful studio in Hollywood, renown for the glossy, bright, Technicolor style of its films, complete with lavish wardrobes, high priced sets, and an unbeatable stable of superstars.

On the one day I was on the set at MGM for the filming of "Soylent Green", I had to report there at six o'clock in the am until approximately one o'clock in the afternoon.

I remember being totally at awe with the set and surroundings. I never saw such an abundance of food in my life, with every type of nourishment man can imagine. There were only brief moments of filming then time was called on the set and there were long pauses when the cast could have refreshments.

I never saw such an accumulation of settings: furniture, curtains, chairs, tables, etc. Many movies and TV shows were filmed there, Ozzie and Harriet, Gone With the Wind, the Wizard of Oz and the like.

****

Connie Williams This Life: Through
Grace Hope and Mercy

The hair style referred to as stunning by D'UrVille Martin.

Photo by Bob More

One day I received an unexpected telephone call and Bob Moore was on the line. He soon revealed, "You're a cover girl Sweetheart," using sweetheart as a term of endearment.

Connie Williams   This Life: Through
                    Grace Hope and Mercy

Portfolio photograph taken by Bob Moore

Connie WilliamsThis Life: Through
Grace Hope and Mercy

Photo by Bob Moore

Connie Williams   This Life: Through Grace Hope and Mercy

A final Letter of communication to me from Bob Moore in October 1985. I had moved back to North Carolina:

Dear Connie,

In spite of the extreme brevity of your note, it was a pleasant surprise hearing from you and to know that you, after so long, still allow me to cross your mind. It's annoying, however, that as long as you and I have known one another, you find so little to say to me.

Judging by the picture you sent, you're still cute. But who took that picture? Aren't there any good photographers in North Carolina?

I'm glad you're getting along okay.

But, how can you teach English, when you don't even write any details about the level of English, nor do you tell about the grade level of your students. But if you had given those details, I wouldn't have had anything to tease you about.

My situation is pretty much the same. I'm still operating my studio and still teaching photo classes at L.A Southwest College. Business has been very slow for quite a while.

I'm writing a column for a new Compton newspaper in which I give photo tips. In fact, "Photo Tips" is the name of my column. The newspaper, the Compton Inquirer, is not yet off the ground. I hope it makes it.

Starting January 11, I will be teaching a series of 6-week photo classes at a camera store in Los Angeles. Cost of the course will be $150.00. I expect to have at least twenty students per session. There will be a winter, spring, summer, and fall session.

A couple of years ago, I formed a corporation called the Photo Culture Calendar Corporation. Our purpose was to visit a

different country each year and produce a pictorial calendar of the particular country showing the land, monuments, and peoples.
We worked with the concept for about a year; but, like so many good ideas, it fell apart.
My social life has been slow for quite a while. I've been staying close to home. Guess I'm getting older and wiser.
And speaking of older, I'll be a proud and healthy 60 in about 4 months.
If you decide to write me again, please try to find more to say.
I wonder if I will ever see you again.
How are your daughters getting along? Where are they now?
Take care of yourself.
Love,
Bob

Bob never knew that I lost my daughter Dawn in 1984. Telling him would just have been too painful for me and broken my heart. So, I neglected to include that. God knows I sincerely wanted to tell him.

In a letter sent to me from Mrs. A. Vaughnette Moore, Bob's wife, on February 15, 1988, I learned of Bob Moore's passing the year before in 1987. She sent a photo, a South West College Newspaper including Bob's story and his obituary.

She wrote: Dear Connie,

Bob left us many beautiful memories. I am happy that you are a part of them.

The picture of Bob that we used was the last picture he had taken. It is special because it was taken by our son Brandon, who is an artist and a

Connie Williams   This Life: Through Grace Hope and Mercy

photographer. The obituary was written by our daughter Karen. She also conducted the memorial service. Karen is becoming a very good writer and photographer.

Love to you and your family,
Vaughnette Moore

Mr. Robert Moore of Bob Moore Photography in Hollywood, CA who I idolized and respected like a father.

Photo by Anthony Riley, a Southwest College student and Bob Moore protégé

In Hollywood I joined the Autography Modeling School to try and advance an acting career. On the one hand, I somewhat had caught the Hollywood fever, wanting to be a part of the glitz and excitement especially because of how those in the industry responded to my looks, but on the other hand I was completely aware of my responsibilities and commitments. To stay "in the know" I sometimes attended acting classes with a friend, professor Burwell, (Jon's cousin) from the university's wife, who was a tall, European looking woman endeavoring to achieve a modeling contract. These On Method Acting classes were taught by Phillip Roye, the actor from the movie the "Learning Tree." My objective was for the same purpose—to advance a career. I figured if I did land a part in some movie, I felt I should at least know a little about acting. These involvements occasionally placed me in Hollywood and Los Angeles areas. But it was the 70s and life seemed free and harmless. I had not encountered any dangers, so I felt I would be all right because I took the necessary precautions to remain safe—I had purchased my first automobile as soon as we moved to the Valley, and the Volkswagen Bug ran fine; the tires were in good condition; and the gas tank was full. I didn't go drinking at bars nor fractionizing with strangers.

The day before a detrimental Los Angles incident, I had been called by a photographer who was associated with the Modeling school. He and his brother requested that I should come to their apartment for a photo shoot. It didn't feel right for some reason; therefore, I decided I wouldn't go.

I later determined that I didn't want to miss out on the next opportunity to pose for a reputable photographer. So, I met with Anthony R. for a photo shoot—everything went exceptionally well; besides he was a friend and protégé of Bob Moore.

On the evening leaving the engagement and, on the way, home back to the Valley, approximately, 8:00 pm, just about dark I was stopped at a stop light on North Van Ness Avenue, Hollywood.

Before the red light changed to green, I suddenly felt my car door being snatched opened. I heard a voice, and shrieked at the face and eyes of a rough, burly beard black man when he said, "Gemmy all your money or I'll shoot!" He simultaneously pressed a 38-caliber revolver against my temple.

I held onto the steering wheel with one hand; with a trembling right hand I reached into the back seat and pulled my purse to my lap as quickly as I could. Pulling a hand full of change out of the purse, I handed it to the robber.

His large hand over-powered mine, as he reached inside the car to grab the money from my timid, trembling hand with his left hand as he still pointing the gun at my temple with his right. Simultaneously he blurted out an indignant insult, "Ah you ain't got no money!" Afterwards, he slammed the car door shut as if to force it from its hinges. He immediately ran past the back of my car crossed the street, and I saw him dart around the corner disappearing into the night of west Los Angeles.

I managed to lock the car door, put the straight drive of the Volkswagen in first gear and sped off as quickly as the car would go. With my mind in total disbelief—uncertainty of what had just occurred and amazed that I was still alive I believe I cried all the from Hollywood to home in the Valley.

Besides crying, all the way home that night, as I drove from Hollywood to the Valley, I turned the words over and over in my mine, "I could have been killed. I could have been killed. A hole could have been blown through my head--shot to death and left lying on the side of the road or carried somewhere into the Canyons and left there."

> Once again God showed me what
> He is willing to do. Right now, I find myself
> speaking His language of Faith and Grace.
> Leviticus: (NIV) The fruit of an exceptional
> God. (Leviticus 1) And the Lord called unto
> Moses, and spake unto him out of the

tabernacle of the congregation, saying, Speak unto the children….

I'm not sure how soon I dropped out of modeling school and abandoned the idea of acting classes, but I don't recall ever going back to either one. Besides, in the weeks that followed the burly robber kept creeping into my dreams, and mentally showing up in the back seat of my car.

Chapter 7

∞

Driving from the Valley to Los Angeles Trade Tech College proved to be too stressful for me, I was especially cautious after the Hollywood scare. Now I particularly needed to make a change after my Volkswagen broke down on the 405 San Diego Freeway driving home in five o'clock traffic. God sent angels in the form of two white men who rescued me.

God was watching. He will take care of you. (Book of Genesis: Chapter 21)

They pulled their vehicle over in the extreme left lane behind my car and yelled to me, "Get in this car!"

Although I wasn't sure if it was the right thing to do, there wasn't much time for pondering over should I or shouldn't I. Yes, I was frightened, but I wasn't nearly as afraid of them as I was of being stuck in the treacherous five o'clock 405 Freeway traffic. Recently, now on the TV show 20-20 there was a story of a young woman broken down on the 210 Freeway in CA, after a couple stopped to help her. When she never returned home, her body was found in some isolated area along the Canyon road in the Valley.—So I'm glad I jumped into the back seat, and allowed them, who immediately drove me to the nearest Shell station where I used a payphone to call friends of Jon, George and his wife May who came right away to pick me up. Later that night George and Jon fixed the car and drove it to my apartment.

Again, I was blessed and I believe
I was saved.

So many times, I have driven alone and along the long and crowded lanes of the Harbor Freeway, the San Diego, the Hollywood and Santa Monica highways in the big state of California constantly looking around, always looking over my shoulder-- out there without human companionship or protection but with Godly presence.

Shortly after getting the car back, at the end of the academic year and completion of the Stenography course and graduation from Los Angeles Trade Tech College, I soon learned that typists and office assistance jobs weren't paying much money. I needed a four-year degree for my worth to increase, so I transferred to a Valley college, Los Angeles Van Nuys Community College and I changed my major to English.

Graduation

I am second from the left; my graduation photo from Los Angeles Trade Tech College in Stenography not very long after moving to the Valley.

Chapter 8

∞

*I*ronically, with all the beauty I knew, and all of the positive influences in my life, God did not forsake me even when I committed another terribly unwise and unsafe act out of rage.

Grace was sent by God to save me from a life in prison from what would have been considered pre-meditated murder! Although it didn't start out that way, but the end results would have been the same.

God will bless you when you're right and bless you when you make the wrong turn.
God painted a new masterpiece. For

> we are God's masterpiece; He has created us anew in Christ Jesus, so we can do the good things he planned for us long ago. (Ephesians 2:10) NLT.

After my episode with the twenty-two Caliber one would think that it would be enough to scare me into putting that weapon away. But NO! Jon and I, by now, had become very close friends. But he didn't enjoy seeing the Hollywood stars and entertainers possibly getting involved in movies with me, especially a big named actor like Jim Brown. He began to show great jealousy and anger at the idea of the meetings, photo shoots and socialization (which was to a minimum—after all, how much time could I possibly have raising four children and hitting the books as a college student—really)!

Although Jon never ever directed any type of personal contact violence toward me, he had been raised well in a home by two loving parents who lived in Los Angeles, and he had wonderful relatives, aunts, uncles and cousins in the San Fernando Valley, like the professor at the university and his wife, but there were many other ways he showed his disapproval of the "Hollywood" involvement with an endeavor to control my life.

He had first become envious of the meeting I had between D'UrVille Martin and Jim Brown at the Candy Store. (Ironically, I made the decision to take him to the meeting with me because I didn't want to be in Hollywood at night alone at the Candy Store Dance club). At the meeting, while Jim Brown,

D'UrVille and I sat on the bottom step talking about Brown's up-coming film, "The Slams", if my memory serves me correctly, I believe Fred 'the Hammer' Williamson sat on an upper step. Jon sat three steps above us, and from time to time, he could be heard uttering profanity—muttering quietly and indistinctly foul language—the equivalent of "Skubala" used by Apostle Paul. (Philippians 3:8) "Shhh-it." It was totally embarrassing. He was completely out of control with envy.

Scripture is very clear that we are to not let any foul language cross our lips (Exodus 20:7, Ephesians 4:29).

But I suppose Jon just couldn't control his envy. For only a short while afterwards, one day he asked me, "Why are you like that, Man?"

A few days later, Jon was angered by something trivial that escapes my memory, probably obsessed by the idea that I was attempting to follow the dream Bob Moore carried for me to get cast in Jim Brown's movie.

The girls were not home from school yet to see it, so again he chose to allow his anger to get loose, to act like a child and tear down my expensive Harmon Cordon stereo turntable that sat on cinder blocks in the living room. He shoved it causing it to tumble to the floor and then he abruptly left my apartment.

When he left, I got into my Volkswagen and drove to the apartment building on Reseda Boulevard in the Valley where he lived near Northridge. I found his gold Oldsmobile, Toronado, parked underneath the building in the provided parking space. I took the twenty-two Caliber and fired shots that sounded like bombs exploding as I aimed one at a time at each of his four Firestone tires and blew them out and then stepped lightly but hurriedly back into my Volkswagen and left the scene heading for Van Nuys Boulevard.

    Thanks to God, before I could return home, a police car caught up with me before turning off Reseda Boulevard. I surely didn't want my children to witness a policeman after me. The officer only had to sound the siren once as I pulled over on the side of Reseda Boulevard.

    A tall, stout, tanned Euro American officer got out of the police car and came over to where I sat in my vehicle pulled off the street with my head lowered in shame.

    "Mam, I need to see your driver's license and registration." He said.

    Without hesitation and without uttering a word I quickly reached into my purse and brought out the documents and handed them to the officer. He took them and returned to his police car to check them out.

    I thought to myself, thank you Lord I'm clean as a whistle, referring to my identification as a graduate from Los Angeles Van Nuys Junior College, a student at Cal State University, Northridge, and an absence of a criminal record. And in the next moment, my mind flashed back to the Glen Oaks incident. Not only had God kept me from killing Jon, He had also miraculously kept the police and any witnesses from seeing the unfortunate alleged crime.

I'm sorry but I have to say it right now, God must have put sleep over the eyes of the shopkeepers, the passerby's, and every customer in shops to prevent them from seeing or hearing the shots being fired—Our God is one bad Motor Scooter! —Again—I mean--a Baaaddd Motor Scooter! I need an Amen!

When the officer returned to my car, he said, "Mrs. Sims, I have a complaint from the building manager at Reseda Gardens that you destroyed property and caused a disturbance by shooting a gun." He paused—looking around inside my car. "I want you to SLOWLY HAND ME THE GUN and then follow me to the police station."

I didn't hesitate to 'slowly' hand over the gun. I begged, "I'm so sorry officer, but I didn't hurt anyone."

"Mrs. Sims, you could have hurt someone or you could have hurt yourself. What you did was very dangerous, so I want you to follow me to the station." He paused. "If you're not going to follow me, I'll have to put the handcuffs on you and take you down to the station in the police car. Do you understand?"

I nodded my head, "Yes sir." I cranked the car and when the officer pulled off in the police car, I pulled off right behind him.

When I arrived at the police precinct, parked my car and the officer escorted me in, there sat Jon on a bench veering at me with scornful eyes that peeped out above his hand that partly covered an expression of disgust. I later learned he too had been brought in because his landlord had him arrested for disturbing the peace. Rightfully so, I felt, after all he started this awful mess in the first place when he tried to destroy my property in my home.

A white female officer took me into an area for fingerprinting and background check for police clearance. I was read the Miranda Rights and then fingerprinted. The officer then took me to a section for females in the precinct that resembled a shower and asked me to bend over and spread my gluteus maximus— my buttock, in search of hidden drugs I'm sure, and then she went through every inch of the contents in my purse. I wasn't interrogated per se, but I too, was detained, yet neither Jon nor I was put into a cell. After the female officer returned my purse, she left both of us alone, Jon and me, sitting in chairs in close proximity in the police precinct lobby.

Of all things, Jon tried to talk to me as we sat there, "Now look at what you've done!" He accused me.

I didn't respond. As a college senior, I learned to keep my mouth shut at times like these. Those officers and authoritative persons wanted us to begin arguing—causing a disturbance at the police station which could lead to further charges; that was all we needed. Even Jon should have logically figured that one out.

After a short while, an officer came to take me into his office to ask me what happened. I explained the situation as completely as possible. Of course, they had already taken the gun.

Then the officer counseled me, "Look Mrs. Sims, you're a college student and going to become a teacher. If something like this gets into the newspaper, it won't do your reputation any good. It could possibly ruin your future opportunities and career goals."

I listened well.

Shortly after the conversation with the officer, we were fined, I don't remember how much, and Jon's Aunt Lynette came for both of us.

In a sermon I recall preached by our own
Dr. Lynch: Covenant partner, Living in redemption. I believe in my heart Jesus is Lord.
A whole life can change through
the response of Grace and Faith.
God painted a new masterpiece. (2 Samuel).

What I soon acknowledged is that 22 Caliber gun would only have ruined my life and kept me from successes. I soon acknowledged also that I needed to take a good long look at my relationship with Jon. Basically, he was a wonderful person, but his jealous flare-ups and impulsive immaturity did not bring out the best in me, which obviously had proven wasn't necessarily good for him either.

Chapter 9

∞

Once again God sent an angel in the form of my daughter Pricilla.
This is very difficult to tell!!!

    Following the conflict with Jon, he and I didn't see each other as often, and eventually, over the next year, naturally we drifted apart. He still would come by to see the girls and me from time to time like Thanksgiving holiday, when he knew I was making a turkey dinner. And he would express a desire for us to continue a relationship, but to no
avail because I felt I had outgrown Jon once I matriculated to the University.

Connie Williams

This Life: Through Grace Hope and Mercy

    Life had always been totally complex and exhausting from my early teenage years until womanhood. In the mists of this complexity there wasn't time to focus upon what wasn't taking place, what I didn't have, what I needed, what I desired. I just had hope that I could maintain—push forward each and every day—keep putting one foot in front of the other—trying to be both mother and father to my children.

    With the responsibilities of my children's needs becoming more complicated, school requirements, there was only time to take care of whatever the issue was and move on because tomorrow was certainly arising with its own life storms: Raise the children, take care that the bills were paid; enough food on the table for four growing teenagers; clothes for them; attend college and write those English papers; pass the test; remain in the top third of the English classes at California State University Northridge.

    The ideology and intention were so that I could land a well-paying job that would raise the standard of living; mainly it was to set an example for my children that if I could educate my mind for a better life, I wanted to show them that they too could do it.

    My children were totally involved with constructive activities: athletics—riding a ten-speed; swimming, running track with the neighborhood Girls and Boys Club; academically—the Gifted and Talented program; writing plays and participating in

Drama, acting in Kennedy High School Drama, Speech Delivery contest, attending the plays at the local theater, Van Nuys College and Kennedy High School. It was at this time that I enrolled my oldest daughter but, the youngest contestant at age thirteen, in the Hal Jackson's Foxes and Hares Miss Black Teenage San Fernando Valley Beauty Contest organized by Maria Foley.

FOXES AND HARES "Black Teenage California" pageant at the International Hotel recently was well received. Left to right, Bill Howard, pageant director, with winners Robin Belinda Sims (Miss San Fernando Valley), Jo Ann Renata Ford (Miss Monterey Peninsula) and bin Mitchell (Miss San Bernardino). Ford, pageant title winner, now go New York for the national finals of Hal Jackson "Miss Black Teenage A ca" pageant to be held July 27.

Connie Williams   This Life: Through Grace Hope and Mercy

Newspaper article: Los Angeles Sentinel Newspaper

Not only was Raven the winner of Miss Black Teenage San Fernando Valley contest, she became the first runner up to the California State finals.

It was at this time that I met the late Michael Evens from the TV show "The Jefferson's." He was the Master of Ceremony at the contest when Raven won the Miss Black Teenage San Fernando Valley beauty contest. This photo was taken at Michael Evens home in the Hollywood Hills, California.

    To prepare for the contest, obviously, I could not be in every place and I did not have eyes in the back of my head. I did not have a relative to turn to for help in times of frustration and despair. Raising the four children and being totally responsible for every need, to say the very least, was always physically and mentally exhausting, and I was still a student at Cal State University, Northridge.

There were rehearsal schedules and deadlines to meet (photo shoots) to attend "on time" performance attire and gowns to purchase, hair to style and still take care of the needs of my other three children while all of this was going on.

> **But God** is faithful; he **will not** allow you to be tempted beyond what you are able. He **will not** let you be tempted **more than** you **can bear**. At the time you are **put** to the test, He **will** give you the strength to endure it. (Corinthians 10:13).

Besides my daughter Raven's winning these titles: Miss San Fernando Valley, and the first runner-up to the California State Finals, she and her sisters were in the process of establishing a sibling singing group: "S" Incorporated.

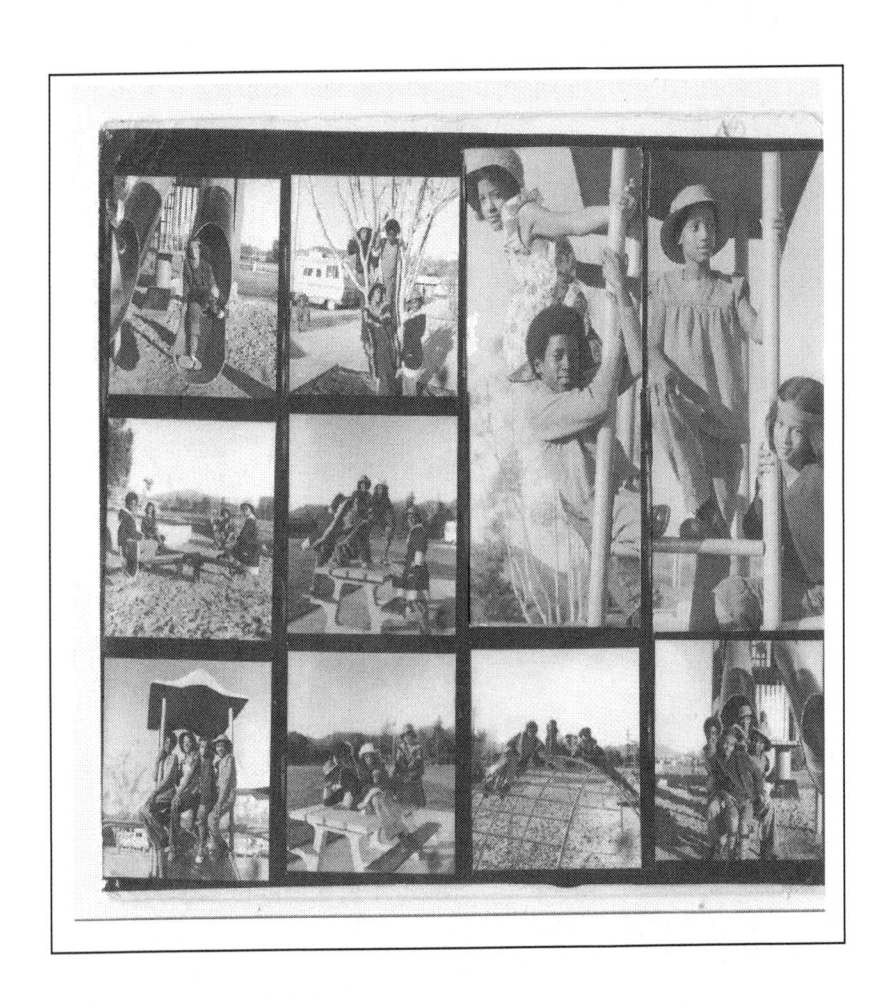

Sims Incorporated photo shoot: Fillmore Street Park, San Fernando Valley, CA. Photo by "Lafayette."

Photo by Lafayette, San Fernando Valley, CA

    Sims Inc. had rehearsals on Saturday mornings in Hollywood with Karl Jones, the same vocal trainer for the Fifth Dimensions, an American, Grammy Award winning popular musical group. In fact, the Fifth Dimensions would be leaving the studio just as the "S" Incorporated and I were arriving. The lessons were expensive and sponsored for us by the children's Uncle James.

    The schedules were overwhelming. So finally, I found a vocal coach closer in Northridge to where we lived in the Lake View Terrace/Pacoima area. But James (the uncle) wasn't willing to allow the group to switch coaches—he wasn't willing to pay for a coach that was unfamiliar and that he himself had not chosen.

And after a while, we began rehearsals at home. I began to coach the group and they performed at local hotel events and backyard, around the swimming pool invites in the Valley.

I so much wanted the singing group to be successful as much as I thought they did. But sometimes at the swimming pool events, they were reluctant to sing. I began to practice the girls hard. I somewhat became as regimented as Jo Jackson with his sons, the Jacksons Five, but not as strict and absent of the use of abuse. When I took the group on auditions, they sometimes didn't want to audition. My girls decided they only wanted their oldest sister to take charge of the practices. They were children, they wanted to ride their ten-speed bicycles—they wanted to go to parties and socialize with friends— they wanted to spend more time playing. And the singing group before long as far as any seriousness was concerned soon consequently became a dream of the past.

These events are so very difficult to recount. In the meanwhile, I received my Bachelor's Degree in English in December, one semester early in 1978 from Cal State University, Northridge. I was exhausted, to put it mildly. I couldn't laugh, cry, scream or any of those emotions. I was just totally exhausted and wanted to rest—to lie down and go to sleep for at least a week. I took some of the pills issued out by the Cal State University doctors. The angel Pricilla found me sleeping; she called for help.

> God sent Mercy to save me once again!
> God forgives 70 times 170; He takes care of babies and foolish individuals.

Chapter 10

∞

*I*n **1978 following the breakdown,** I moved back to North Carolina with my youngest daughter Camille and Larry my first-born's father. Before we left California, my oldest daughter at eighteen had already flown to NC to live with her grandmother and complete her senior year in high school. Pricilla at seventeen wanted to remain in Los Angeles with her father; and Dawn at age sixteen, poor little girl, was so full of life and once she became sixteen, she would not attend school on a regular basis. So frequently I would receive calls from the school that she wasn't in her classes, and I would have to literally comb the neighborhood finally locating her at some friend's house without my permission. After much effort to get her to follow my rules, Dawn was so smart and reminded me that she could become an emancipated teenager. California laws state that children must generally be 14 years of age or older in order to be eligible to become emancipated, (where a minor is no longer legally under the care of his or her parents). Consequently, at sixteen she decided to try the benefits of completing her high school education in the Job Corp Program in Texas. I believe Dawn was attracted to the idea that students would receive a living allowance to attend the classes. According to the research, the program offered career technical training in more than 100 career areas. Students receive housing, meals, basic health care, a living allowance, training, and preparation for a career, all at no cost. I tried convincing her otherwise, but to no avail. This is another extremely difficult period in my life.

Nonetheless, once it seemed the girls were situated, I made the move with hopes to start a better life in North Carolina with Larry. One wouldn't think so judging by his family background, but God soon revealed to me that Larry's intentions were less than honorable once we returned to North Carolina, but at the onset, how was I to know. I had NOT focused upon, in the words of Marvin Gaye: "What's Going On" in North Carolina with Larry—I was too busy with what was going on in our lives on the West Coast. I was in no way prepared or of actually being aware of Larry's life over the years; I had totally been out of touch with him until after my divorce from Walter and the hundreds of love letters, over a period of a year, Larry wrote to me with his intentions of convincing me to give him another chance. My awareness of him was that he was my oldest child's father who I did not marry, but instead at age fifteen married Walter his best friend.

I knew that Larry came from very respectful and fine upstanding professional parents from Monroe, my home town. How could someone with such a protective background be all bad? Once he made his initial contact with me right before I graduated from Cal State Northridge, he began writing many love letters confessing that he had gotten into trouble, but testifying that he was older now and much wiser; and he wrote about how he had totally turned his life around. In his letters, his endeavor was to convince me that he had never in fact gotten over our relationship. In other words, he confessed in his letters that in the deepest part of his heart, he was still in love with me after all these years.

At this particular time in my life, as an escape mechanism to a more pleasant state of mind, in my dreams, I sometimes eluded to this romantic story-book idea held in my head about our future based on some literature I may have read:

[Now in turn Chip=LB-the son of Grace stepped off the plane held Constance=Connie in his arms and whispered love.

But in reality, Constance made her light-footed way to the place of incarceration. And Chip, handsome as the morning sun saw her, and when he saw her desire was a mist about his close heart as much as on that time they first fell into each other's arms and stood in love, and their dear parents knew nothing of it. He stood before her and called her by name and spoke to her: What is your desire that you came down here to the South from the West? And your children are not here, nor your automobile, which you would ride in?

Then with false lying purpose, the lady Constance answered him. I am going to the end of the generous earth, on a visit to Monroe to see my parents who brought me up kindly in their own house, and cared for me. I shall go there and resolve their division of discord, since now for a long time they have been quarreling and have stayed apart from each other and from the bed of love.

Then in answer Chip the handsome, who gathered the rays of the sun said, "Constance, there will be time after when you can go there as well. But now let us go to bed and turn to love-making. For never before has love for any girl or woman so melted about the heart inside me; broken it to submission as now: not like the time when I loved the wife of Sabrith who bore me Lamar Jr., equal to all the young men of his age, nor when I loved Bell's daughter, a sweet stepping girl; nor when I loved the daughter at Livingstone.

Chip's mind recalled when he loved the wife of Sabrith, who bore him a son, and how David seduced his neighbor Bathsheba. She became pregnant. So, he brought to memory how his best friend had long ago taken his girl. He had never truly gotten over it. Bathsheba's husband was at the battlefront, fighting one of his skirmishes. She let LB know that she had become pregnant by him. Chip like David thought this mess might yet be covered up by his running away.

Then she brought him now to the present; again, with false lying purpose the lady answered: What sort of thing have you spoken? If now your great desire is to lie in love together, here on the hard cots where everything can be seen, then what would happen if someone of the guards saw us sleeping and went and told all the others of it? I would not simply rise out of bed and go back again to the West, and, such a thing would be shameful. No, if this is your wish, if this is your heart's desire then there must be another way.

Then LB who gathered the rays of the sun answered: Con. Do not fear that any person or any friend will see, so close shall be the golden cloud that I gather about us. Not even "Big Red" (a friend and benevolent, poetry writing inmate) who towers 6 feet tall and 6 inches, and can look over it.

Then speaking the son of Grace caught his beloved in his arms. There underneath them the divine earth broke into young fresh grass, and into dewy clover, crocus and hyacinths so thick and soft it held the hard cot deep away from them. Then they lay down together and drew about them a golden wonderful cloud, and from it the glimmering dew descended. And the son of Grace slept unshaken on a cloud with his love in his arms, when sleep and passion had stilled him. Constance turned softly and smiled to have him sleeping in love beside her. The gentle sleep of the couple so sweet that all around them began to heavy with want of slumber—the eyelids; and everything was right with their world. Was this a new beginning?]

> I need to admit right here and now,
> I knew God at a young early age.
> But once I became a student matriculating
> in the academia, I began to drift away
> from my upbringing.

After becoming aware of the many schools of thought and philosophies, I began to question God: Creation Vs Evolution; Darwin's argument of evolution through natural selection; especially, Man and free will. Are faith and belief in evolution necessarily at odds? <u>According to Pope Francis</u>, the answer is no. Indeed, the pope recently reaffirmed the Roman Catholic Church's view that "evolution in nature is not inconsistent" with church teaching on creation, pushing the <u>debate on human origins</u> back <u>into the news</u> now in the 21st Century.

According to research, the rejection of evolution by most evangelicals is largely mirrored by their churches, such as the <u>Southern Baptist Convention</u> and the <u>Lutheran Church-Missouri Synod</u>, which explicitly reject evolutionary theory as being in conflict with what they see as biblical truth.

Well, in the 70s, with my 'so called educated and enlightened mind; the free will granted by our Creator began to cause poor choices—turning away from God. I believe it may have been mostly because my life was so hard. And because of that suffering, I just found it difficult to believe that if God loved me, and I continued to make a conscious effort to be a good person—doing what was right by my children, and myself; abiding within the laws, then I just couldn't help but wonder, why is and why should my life be that difficult. Deep down inside, I just wanted God to step in and make it all better—make it easier—help me! It seemed that Larry might be the answer.

What a way to discover that this Larry person was completely and utterly lost. Once we merged in California, there were signs that I ignored. And once we were in North Carolina, I learned that underneath his facade he secretly wanted me to be lost also. My story-book ideas about any future quickly faded away. Obviously, he wanted to wreck my life—after all his certainly was wrecked. Although he was his parents (professional, successful, church going people's) only child, one would never believe the energy and finances that had been made available to help him. He was an *entitled* person. He had been in and out of prison for many years for various reasons including drug addiction, and his parents continued to dote on him like he was a child, and enable him. And he had not changed—this I did not know. There were some subtle little hints seeped out to me from an oldest sister; nevertheless, there was nothing of a serious and "warning nature" information that I would have wished for.

Yet because I was with this person, many that were close to me in my family circle and others who knew Larry stood around watching and waiting because it was hard to believe I had gone into that direction. They didn't want me to lose everything I had accomplished. They didn't want me to be unsuccessful—TO FAIL ALSO—JUST LIKE HE HAD FAILED IN LIFE!

>But what they did not know about
>me was that because I "knew" God
>at an early age, He had shown favor,
>He had saved me to Glorify Him and
>tell this story.

In spite of the negativity Larry brought into my life, God did not allow me to fail. He allowed me to mentally move on with my life; tell Larry as kindly as possible, "You're not the person for me!" I believed it would be a smooth transition, but I was mistaken. For the first time, a side of his personality was revealed that was a surprising threat. I truly believe if my brother had not come running to my rescue, Larry was about to cause detrimental harm to me as we sat in his automobile, after I told him we were through. Our Lord allowed my brother to be in the right place at the right time so that I could move on with my life. The message to Larry I thought had been clear.

Following that experience, I interviewed for a full-time professional position in the school system in Union County.

Once I applied to the school system in Union County, on the day that I interviewed with the Superintendent of the schools, Mr. McCain, he asked, "Connie Williams, do you know a man named Connie Williams?"

I responded, "Well yes, that's my father."

"Well, Lord Have Mercy; your father has repaired every chair in my house! I can still hear your brothers fussing at him for working too hard." He said.

Following my interview, I was hired for the academic year at Piedmont High School which led to a career of fifteen successful years. While teaching there, Larry again begin writing love letters asking to see me so that we could talk. Of course, I had better sense than to fall for his deceit. So finally, after a time when I never responded, he finally gave up and the letters stopped.

While at Piedmont, my teaching career was full of numerous responsibilities. I was nominated twice for the prestigious title as Teacher of the Year, and a Christa McAuliffe Fellow finalist.

Connie Williams   This Life: Through Grace Hope and Mercy

Piedmont teacher uses her book to work with students

By Beverly Brock, Staff Writer

Writing a novel called "Emily's Blues" has brought much joy and excitement into the life of Piedmont High School teacher Connie Williams.

It has taken 19 years and probably 25 rewrites to complete it, she said, but it's been worth it.

Because of her efforts, some of her students are performing a play called "Emily's Dilemma," adapted from Williams' book, today at Livingstone College. It's a part of the Emily's Blues Self Actualization Project, a program Williams designed to work with her students.

The book is about a girl, who marries young, moves away from her family, has children and becomes abused by her husband. She travels from North Carolina to New Jersey and eventually to California.

"It's a young girl growing up and dealing with a lot of adversities and persevering to overcome some of those adversities," Williams said. "Most of all, it's saying it doesn't matter where you come from, it's where you're going that counts."

It's a good story for teens to learn from, she said, and her students create their own stories from it. The group of her 11th- and 12th-graders were asked to give a performance at Livingstone College in Salisbury.

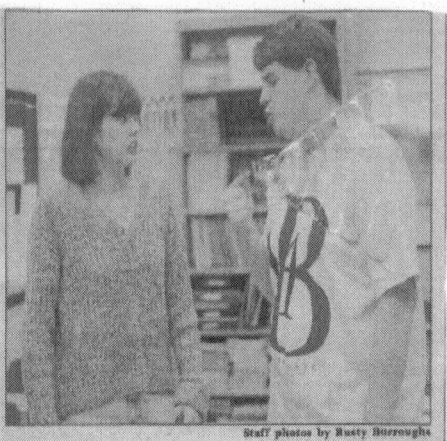

Writing the story is something that has brought many opportunities to Williams. Her latest opportunity will be this summer as she was chosen to participate at the Headlands Center for the Arts in Sausalito, Calif.

Based on her final revisions of the book, Williams will go to the center from June 7 to Aug. 12. Her trip is funded through a grant with the North Carolina Arts Council and the National Endowment for the Arts.

"They want you to come fresh and clear and start something there," Williams said. "I will be writing. I will write for two months — interact with other artists, which I am looking forward to. They just want us to be inspired and create.

"I'm hoping to collaborate with some of the other artists there," she said. "I do write poetry, and I have some ideas for some stage plays. There's a lot going in this head."

For years, Williams tried to get her novel published. "I have at least two whole file drawers of rejections, and I

Please see Project on 2A

Staff photos by Rusty Burroughs
Robin Parker, left, and Travis Ray practice their parts for the play they are performing today in Salisbury.

    I founded the Emily's Blues Self-Actualization Project, an arts education program designed to deter student dropouts, featuring student tutors and Piedmont's first ever drill team that performed at home games, and they represented the school in the Monroe Christmas parade. The Union County Community Arts Council funded the program for several years until I decided to transfer to Charlotte Mecklenburg Schools where I resided.

    God had my back. Teaching school is difficult/hard work even with the best students, great colleagues and the excellent resources. Additionally, to teaching English, Social Studies, US History and Economic, Legal and Political Systems, I was also a cheerleader coach. Talk about long hours. Not only did I have the responsibility of presiding over the girls home and away games, but it was also necessary for me to take them to camp during the summer for training.

> Only God could have brought me through such grueling and rigorous responsibilities. I asked him each morning to direct my feet toward the right path. Establish my footsteps according to your word. (Psalm 119:133).

Although the work was laborious, and I wore several hats for several roles, it was so enjoyable. I had incredible students, who were delighted when engaged in unique and different activities additional to the mundane traditional lessons or studying history and writing. For instance, we burned in a fire-lit barrel the concept of "I Can't" at a funeral memorial on the Piedmont campus where the entire faculty including the principal participated. We formed the Wacky-Pack Corporation to study the Universal Law of Supply and Demand. My students bought a one dollar share into the company. Student who arrived at school and did not have the proper supplies came to us to purchase pencils and paper for fifty cents. The profits were used to celebrate the end of the semester with a Pizza party.

J. Cross who was our high school principal at the time was invited to come to the classroom to witness us demonstrate the ULOSAD. He responded, "I'll help you demonstrate the law. Send me some Pizza!"

During that same time, I wrote a stage play, "Emily's Dilemma", based on the novel *Emily's Blues,* and the students performed it at school and we were invited to Livingston College where they performed it as well. The Union County Community Arts Council funded EBSAP. These funds allowed us to invite M. Macon a Charlotte, NC writer, who taught scoring a play; and Dr. C. Hayes directed our play.

While celebrating African American History month, our students read and studied works by famous and noteworthy African Americans. Mr. F. Terry the vice principal who once lived in Kuwait, (Kuwait is situated northeast of Saudi Arabia at the northern end of the Persian Gulf, south of Iraq), we collaborated to display Kenya and Tanzania artifacts and cultural exhibits in the library. My arts-educational project, EBSAP sponsored a Book Fair "Meet the Authors" and eight African American writers displayed their works and spoke with our students about writing in the Piedmont library.

We took field trips: to the Botanical Gardens at Discovery Place. My mother was kind enough to attend as a chaperone; when we loaded the bus to return home, a homeless man living on the streets of Charlotte, NC boarded the bus and sat down right beside my mom. I went to the beggar and simply asked him, "Will you please get off this bus?" The transient man simply got up and stepped light-footedly down the bus steps and onto the sidewalk, disappearing around the corner of Trade and Seventh.

The students, some of my colleagues, my assistant and I saw the stage play "The Canterbury Tales" at Sprit Square, and students were thrilled when the announcer called me to the stage to participate as an extra in the Nun's Priest's Tale.

My students literally ate a Barbecue Restaurant out of business at their 'all you can eat' ribs on Tryon Street where they practiced reading and ordering from a menu.

I began teaching school in the late 70s at a time when reel-to-reel projectors were used to show a film in the classroom that sometimes broke right in the middle of the movie. And I retired when all we had to do was pop a CD Rom into a computer or computer tablet and tap on an icon on a screen to prompt the start function. Also, I retired at a time when students put together multimodals: multiple modes of interacting with a system and providing several distinct tools for input and output, as their final projects.

God blessed me to teach some of the finest high school and college students in the world, and even today after so many years following my retirement in 2014, they still come running to me and hugging whenever they see me out and about.

Connie WilliamsThis Life: Through
Grace Hope and Mercy

High school and college students at work.

Connie Williams

This Life: Through Grace Hope and Mercy

Amazing students from my English classes at Charlotte-Mecklenburg: Larry Crowder, former Chef at Golden Corral; Markeeyah Lowery, CEO at Rapid Tax. Hugo at the Little Rock Literary Festival 2017 (Mascot).

Chapter 11

∞

God sent Mercy in the form of a male angel to save me who happened to be sitting in his automobile in front of the Tryon strip mall in north Charlotte. He was waiting for his wife while she shopped.

One afternoon after driving from Piedmont High School to Mecklenburg County from work, at about dusk dark, I stopped to shop at the strip mall on Tryon Street and Eastway Drive in north Charlotte. I wanted to pick up a gift card to give to a fellow colleague, whose son was graduating the next day. Therefore, I had walked around in the store for a short while to select the card, gotten in line to pay the clerk for the card. I strolled nonchalantly to my Mazda parked not too far away in the store parking lot. As I approached my automobile, I did notice a silver gadget underneath my driver's side tire. Instinctively I kicked the silver object away from the car, unlocked the door and climbed inside. Placing the key in the ignition I cranked the car put the gearshift in drive and began to mash the accelerator, but the car would not move. I mashed the accelerator harder and still the car would not move. It seemed to be obstructed by something preventing it at the back tire. I panicked, and my instincts told me that I was in danger. I began honking the horn as hard as I could and yelling "Help! Help me!" out of the window to let someone know there was a problem.

As it turned out the gentleman who was waiting for his wife in front of the store heard the honking horn and the motor of my car being rushed; he jumped from his car and ran over to where I was parked.

Consequently, a man had been lying on the ground on the passenger side of my car. He jumped up and ran away as the man who came to my rescue chased after him. Although the gentleman was unable to catch up with this perpetrator before he managed to reach his car and escape, he was able to get the license plate number to provide it for the police.

Shortly afterwards, I received a summons to appear in court. Before the court case, the wife of the culprit, who identified herself as a nurse at CMC

Hospital called me. This was quite disturbing because it was hard to believe that the police department had made my telephone number available to her.

The purpose for her call, she said, was to plead with me about bringing any charges against her husband. She went on to confess, "My husband experienced a difficult upbringing but he has worked hard to try and turn his life around; he's a deacon in the church and a good man."

I was tempted to ask, "Do good men stalk females; attempt to scare females—possibly attempt to abduct them?" But I didn't ask. I was too afraid to stir up any confrontational debate with this stranger who was talking to me on the telephone. She knew how to reach me. But she was totally a mysterious stranger to me. Actually, she could have been anyone pleading for him.

Over the next few days arriving home from work, I was constantly looking over my shoulders. I learned from the information provided in the summons that the man's name was Randall S and he lived in the neighboring apartment in north Charlotte. And on some nights, I found myself double checking the locked doors and windows.

On the day of the trial, for the first time, I came face to face with the man who had been lying on the ground next to my car. He was waiting in the courtroom lobby, and I was terrified! Not by the way he looked because his appearance was like many well-dressed Christian males—suit and tie polished, well groomed. What was horrifying was the flashback to the day of the incident. Of course, my mind conjured up the worst thoughts: I could have been abducted, killed and my body later found in the woods somewhere. I didn't want to have to look at him so I moved down the hall away from his presence.

The gentleman who rescued me was also waiting in the lobby of the courtroom when I arrived. We simply exchanged "Hello and how have you been? Thank you for what you did. You're welcome."

When the hands on the clock reached their home at nine, when I was to appear; I soon entered the courtroom with trepidation. The court bailiff carried out his motion to us, and I heard our names called: Mrs. Williams Vs Randal S. There were three charges against Randal S.: 1] Statue: NCGS 14-277.3A Stalking: Unwanted or obsessive attention by an individual or group towards another person. Stalking behaviors are related to harassment and intimidation and may include **following** the victim in person or monitoring them (McManus 2017). 2] Statue: NCGS 14-3a: False imprisonment: Obstructing the movement of my automobile, by placing two objects in two locations, one under the front tire on the driver's side, and placing an object under the rear tire on the passenger's side (McManus 2017). Punishment of misdemeanors, infamous offenses, offenses committed in secrecy and malice, or with deceit and intent to defraud, or with ethnic animosity. 3] Causing fear and allegedly attempted to do harm by lying on the ground and hiding beside my vehicle.

There was the eye witness, who testified to coming to my rescue when he heard me screaming, while I struggled to drive off—when the car was prevented from moving. The witness also testified to seeing the man lying on the ground on the passenger side of my vehicle. The man lying on the ground did not run away until I honked my horn and yelled for help and the gentleman approached my car to help me. Then and only then did the culprit jump up and run away.

Randal S. admitted following me around in the store before placing those objects underneath my tires. When asked what his intentions were, he claimed he didn't plan to hurt me. Truthfully, I didn't press charges that may have resulted in incarceration, because I was afraid of what he might do to me when he was released. After all, the authorities had made my telephone number available to him when someone called posing as his wife. But I did request that he be assigned community services and that he attend counseling.

Unfortunately, the gentleman who came to my rescue, provided the license plate information and testified was outraged that I didn't want to press charges, and he abruptly left the courtroom in a huff, which I totally understood and could identify with his reaction. I only hope he forgave me if I disappointed him.

Thanks to God and the man who came
to my rescue, I wasn't abducted or hurt,

only frightened half to death. But God
has a way of erasing painful
and frightening experiences.

I've not seen or heard from any of these people after the ordeal—the gentleman who saved me or the criminal who was lying on the ground who caused my automobile to become immobile. I'm not sure I would recognize them today using any of my senses: sight, touch, smell, hearing, if they were directly facing me.

Since the ordeal, I make a conscious effort to be less naïve and more aware of my surroundings wherever I go. We as responsible individuals should watch as well as pray. I didn't recount to any of my colleagues at Piedmont the details of the unfortunate and terrifying experience.

Chapter 12

∞

On the day I shared with the principal at Piedmont High School where I taught school that I had written a book, *Emily's Blues*, Mr. A. Price immediately telephoned the Union Observer Newspaper and a staff writer appeared on campus to interview me and take my picture standing in front of my classroom door. The next week I made the front page of The Union Observer paper in an article entitled 'It's My Life."

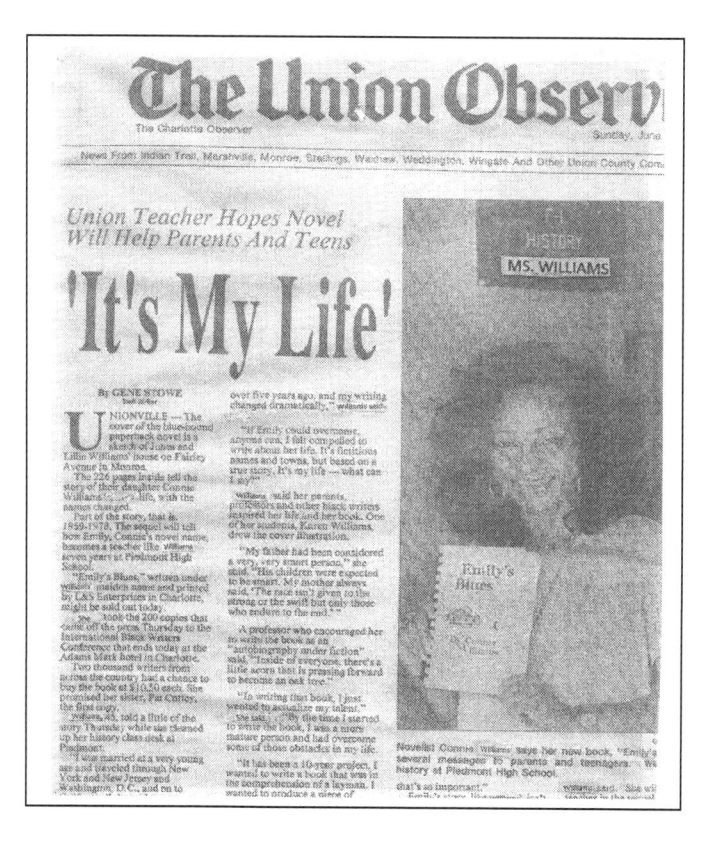

This article was written by Jean Stowe staff writer for the Union Observer.

****

Dr. George Herrick, my college professor from California wrote the following review of *Emily's Blues:*

Connie Williams   This Life: Through
                                   Grace Hope and Mercy

Dear Connie,

<u>Emily's Blues</u> – yes, I like it. Also, I like the absence of self-pity that could have crept in after the mistreatment by Larry and Walter, and to a much less importance, but still significant, intent by Mrs. Honeysuckle, not to mention the omnipresent poverty.

I also like the incisive portrayal of an adolescent's emotions while Emily is in Morristown and first being sought by Larry and later by Walter. Emily's feelings about her home and her family members are also brought out very well as are such welcome details as what the characters wear, the odors of home cooking, and the changes in the weather.

Furthermore, I think that the dialogue is excellent. The people, and you have included a variety of them, speak like people really speak.

I also like the "envelope" or "near envelope" technique that you have used, beginning with, no really following the Prelude, with the report from the Mental Health Center in Mountain View, the letters from Larry, his return and the disastrous aftermath to, at the end, Larry's return to Emily.

Within this "envelope" are the interesting narration and description of Emily's early life in Morristown, the romance with Larry, the marriage to Walter and the experiences in New York, New Jersey, and California.

Another technique that I think is good is the "dream sequence" (pg. 162-177) which provides the reader with valuable glimpses of Emily's past. In this respect the Prelude is also a good introduction to Emily and to her earlier life as well as to her perspectives.

Connie Williams   This Life: Through Grace Hope and Mercy

As an aside, one cameo that I particularly like is your description of Hershey and Hershey's Grill. This is typical of countless high school hangouts and yet unique.

The chief weakness to me is a rather minor one, but one that should not be disregarded. The proofreading could have been done with greater care. While not frequent, errors like the misspelled "senorita," "shiny" (misspelled twice and spelled correctly once) and "Joe Louis" should be reduced and, if possible, eliminated.

All this, of course, is the carping of an aged English teacher. What is not, is my real appreciation for your able depicting of the emotions, aspirations, and experiences of a person who has endured, survived and overcome the nearly crushing adversity of an ill-starred love affair, an unfortunate marriage, and, coincidentally, the incessant struggle against poverty. <u>Emily's Blues</u> describes all this and describes it well.

Thank you again for the privilege of reading it, a really rewarding experience. With my thanks are my very best wishes plus congratulations on that recently earned master's degree. What's next?

                    Sincerely,

                    George Herrick

P.S. * All of this without becoming hopelessly embittered and cynical, GHH.

When Dr. Herrick passed away in 1995, his wife, Betty Herrick, wrote the follow letter:
Dear Ms. Williams,

I regret to inform you that George Herrick is unable to be of further help to you in any of your future projects. George passed away March 19, 1995 of prostate cancer.

Nevertheless, I wish you total success in your new projects. They sound fascinating.

Please forgive me for being the bearer of bad news.

I hope the New Year will bring you joy and success.

*Sincerely,
Betty Herrick*

While teaching at Piedmont High, I met the late and renowned Mr. Alex Haley through the International Black Writers of Charlotte who once told me the story of what becoming a writer is actually like. He confessed, "These words are going to be the best truth and advice, and the best favor I can possibly give." His words were a thunderbolt to my mind!

Mr. Haley was my first mentor. I'm partly sure I learned about him the same way most people did in the late sixties when he wrote the *Autobiography of Malcolm X* and in the seventies when "Roots" was made available on the newsstands and aired on television. I felt and shared the pride that he instilled in all of us through his writing.

I believe that it was along this time in my life that I had read Maya Angelo's book *I know Why the*

Cage Bird Sings and had begun to take my own writing more seriously. I was deeply moved by Ms. Angelou's book because what I read were paralleled experiences to my own life story in many ways. So I believe it was the occurrences of these extraordinary events that I decided to write my own story, partly because writing was a companion to me being a divorced parent and a college student without the time to be involved in much dating, but mostly because I felt that I had a story to tell that would hopefully benefit someone who read it.

Therefore, in the seventies I started to lay out the plan to write my first novel, *Emily's Blues* a fictionalized autobiography.

In 1978 after graduating from Cal State University at Northridge, and after relocating to North Carolina the state of my birth, and beginning a teaching career, it was at this time that I completed a first manuscript and made a conscious decision to try and get it published.

I read in the Charlotte Observer that the North Carolina Writers Network was having Mr. Haley as their key-note speaker at the fall conference. Well, as a novice at this business, I was unfortunately under the assumption that as a writer, my job was to get the words on paper and the editing team that took on the manuscript would work with it and put it in the proper form.

I therefore, released the work to a novice editor that was more or less a typist and we worked together to get the manuscript what should have been press ready. In 1989 the first edition of *Emily's Blues* was self-published in poor condition with hopes that it would be eventually picked up by a publishing house. (My Indie publication experiences is another book that I must write in the near future).

In the meanwhile, I joined a local writing organization, the International Black Writers of Charlotte whose mission was to encourage and display new writing talent, whose executive director was M. Macon at the time. This group of people rallied around my every effort to assist in every way they possibly could in exposure, services and comradeship as a new organization themselves, but they could never do the things that a mentor could do as a professional writer—someone indoctrinated in the process of the "publishing world." But what they did was open the avenue. They introduced my work to Mr. Haley by sending him a copy of the book with a cover letter. The rest was up to me to follow through.

Once my book was sent to Mr. Haley, I followed through with a telephone call. Mr. Haley was very receptive of the call and took the time to locate the book from his stacks of mail that he told me he receives on a daily basis. When Mr. Haley found my book, his words to me were warm and inviting. He said, "Connie Williams, *Emily's Blues*. Okay, Connie Williams." This began our mentoring relationship—communicating by telephone and by letters. Mr. Haley seemed delighted to talk with me and promised to return my call once he had an opportunity to read my book.

In a very short period of time, he kept his promise. I found a letter from Mr. Haley and the copy of my book in my mailbox.

He had taken the time to express his feelings for what he read and made many markings in the book about what to do and what not to do in writing. He included a personal remark. "On page 38," he said in the left margin, "Good paragraphs."

In 1990, before his speaking engagement at the North Carolina Writer's Network Conference in Charlotte, the late Mr. Alex Haley wrote to me and asked me to meet with him at the Radisson Plaza Hotel where he would be staying for the event. The purpose of the meeting was to discuss some ideas about beginning writers and my manuscript **Emily's Blues**.

On this particular Saturday, I left the group of novice writers with whom I had eaten lunch, went to Mr. Haley's suite for our clandestine meeting and knocked on the door. I caught sight of his salt and pepper crown as Mr. Haley opened the door and stood there wearing a light gray, pin-striped three-piece suit displaying an illuminating smile before inviting me in. I recall thinking to myself as I stepped into the room, here is the 21st century's most notarized writer about to do writing chit chat with me, a little girl from where my sister PC would call "Plum Nelly," (completely from the country and nearly out of the world).

His attitude was that of a gentleman and a professional, yet one who was concerned enough to spend some of his valuable time listening to the hopes and dreams of one aspiring writer even though he himself was about to address writers from possibly all over the world.

Before plunging into the waters of the writing world, he asked me if I were hungry because he was about to call to the kitchen to order some dinner. And although I had just eaten, do you think that I was about to pass up an invitation to lunch—break bread—dine—eat some chow with the great Alex Haley? I thought to myself—I think not! Not on your life will I refuse this invitation! I replied meekly, "I could stand a little something."

He confessed to me, "Whenever I check into a hotel, one of the first things I like to do is to go into the kitchen to meet and familiarize myself with the cooks and then the hotel staff." He further said, "I think that it is important to stay in touch with the people who serve others." He picked up the telephone receiver to request two orders of blackened trilogy of chicken, beef and some coffee.

As we sat on opposite sides of the table, in front of the window, the sunlight from outside shined across the room and onto my manuscript, which he held in his hand. He swallowed, sipped coffee, looked at me sternly and asked, "So you want to be a writer? Well, it's like this; it takes work—hard work. It's like going from scratch to becoming a brain surgeon. You have to work, study, and work, and work, and work, and work some more. And then, when your name is on a contract, and you can stand alone, you have accomplished something. But the key is to hang in there." He went on to further say, I read your book; "You really have a story to tell."

At that point in time, I made the mistake that I imagine any new writer wanting to take short cuts might make—the mistake of asking him if he would introduce me to his agent. His reply was a surprise to me.

Mr. Haley took another sip of coffee from the cup he held in his hand. He seemed to be gathering his words. Then he looked sternly into my "wide-awaiting eyes," he said, without hesitation, "You really do have a story to tell, but if I did that, you would be in competition with me."

I almost choked! I asked myself, am I hearing right? Did I just hear Alex Haley say that I had a work worthy of being in competition with his? I know I must have looked awfully silly sitting there grinning from ear to ear. But I just couldn't help myself! I had just been given the highest compliment of a lifetime; given to me by the greatest writer of our time. At that moment, I was on top of the world. Forget about him not being willing to use his influence to get me, so to speak, "in the door." In his way of saying no, he had just given me the inspiration I needed to keep on going—to keep plugging away.

[When you get an opportunity to receive Kudos from a living legend, it doesn't get much better than this— the product of hard work and patience].
Author unknown.

As Mr. Haley chewed on his blackened chicken and a piece of bread that he dipped into the gravy from the beef; he then shared stories about writing love letters for Navy buddies while out at sea and the struggle of finally finding a publisher after about seven years of rejections.

By now my self-worth as a writer was soaring. I thought to myself, if Alex Haley was rejected for such a long period of time, then 'who' am I to think negatively when a publisher returns something. I now realized that this is just a part of the process. Perhaps, after all, no great work is produced over night. I am remembering now, the words of one agent who once told me in a rejection letter: "Even the best writers with the best works, it took years to develop."

Alex Haley spoke passionately of his love for the sea and the productive effect it has on his writing ability while "swaying" over the ocean waves. He talked of his monumental experience when he met the renowned author, James Baldwin (who happens to be one of my favorite writers whose works I spoke about at a reading at Barnes and Noble), whom he met at his Greenwich Village apartment in New York. He confessed, "I heard a knock at the door, and upon answering it there stood the slinky looking Baldwin who glided in like fog and sat on an ottoman with his legs crossed Indian style." Mr. Haley had solicited Baldwin's help in getting published. He added he and Baldwin talked about the business of writing, publication and agents and the whole gambit of the situation in the United States and the African American writer, which he said Baldwin confessed was a difficult task in America, leading him to pick up roots to settle in France. He continued, "And when it was time for Baldwin to leave, I watched for a long time as the great writer walked away from my Village apartment and out of sight. And when Baldwin had gone, I pinched myself to be assured that it had been he (Baldwin) who sat and talked with me in my apartment."

Haley's feelings and actions about Baldwin paralleled my vision of him exactly!

More than anything, the meeting with my idol solidified my idea of being on the right track for how I was going about my own writing practices and processes. It confirmed that writing is hard and lonely for even the best writers; and that it is not an easy thing to do. One must love the profession, one must not give up, and one must stay true to the commitment!

I'm reminded once again of Sidney Poitier's advice that goes, I believe something like this: "Never do an artistic favor for a friend, loan them money, be there for them. You just cannot fake good work—good work will stand the test of time. Success is when an occasional good happens."

Mr. Alex Haley sent a copy of his October 1989 Calendar of itinerary.

OCTOBER 1989

SUNDAY	MONDAY	TUESDAY	WEDNESDAY	THURSDAY	FRIDAY	SATURDAY
1 Wcl Nat'lElec Chicago 8:30A	2	3 W IBM Clev, OH Pm Dpt Knox US Air 1112@10:45 Arv Clev. 1:47P	4 wcl IBM	5 Dpt Clev DL #861 @ 9AM Arv Knox 12: Magnes. Shot	6 UT Vets Oakland Dpt Oaklan USAir	7 RetrWCL Pacific Bell San Ramon 3:30PM
8 Dpt Oak.US	9 Memphis Henning	10	11 CA San Bernar Ontario	12 Univer Sacramento 11:45 AM	13 WCL Tucson 10AM Arv Knox @11PM	14 Museu Homec
15 Museum Homecom Norris Wickendens	16 Doubleday Dayton Chicago@ 8:57PM	17 Doubleday Chicago Arv Detroit 11:45PM	18 Doulebay Detroit NW Minneap @10:37PM	19 Doubleday Minneap	20 Dpt Menn DL#1065 Ark Knox@ Ctr. Unders.	21 Martin Marlett Gene Cl Browny
22 UT Vets Retreat @Farm Thru 10/24	23 Wayne Baker FBI	24 First Ten Bank 4-6 Nashv@5	25 Tom T Hall in Nash/Jack DL#341@10P	26 Mr, HVicks School AM & PM	27 Vicks.,Sch Law Retreat Dean 10/29 Law dinn	28 NNA, Hyatt Regenc
29 Dpt Knox US Air Arv. DC 10:	30 Doubledy Washing. (smiths)	31 Doubleday Boston Arv Knox 7PM		**10/12 Dpt Ontario 5:10P Tucson	10/27 Dpt. Jackson Arv. Atlan 6PM	Get caleDpt

Over the months that followed our meeting, Mr. Alex Haley and I corresponded several times, and he continue to encourage me in a way I never knew that such an important figure and icon like himself would take the time to do. His letters, his calendar of itinerary and a photograph are items of memorabilia kept in a large box and in the storehouse of my memory.

Alex Haley's letters

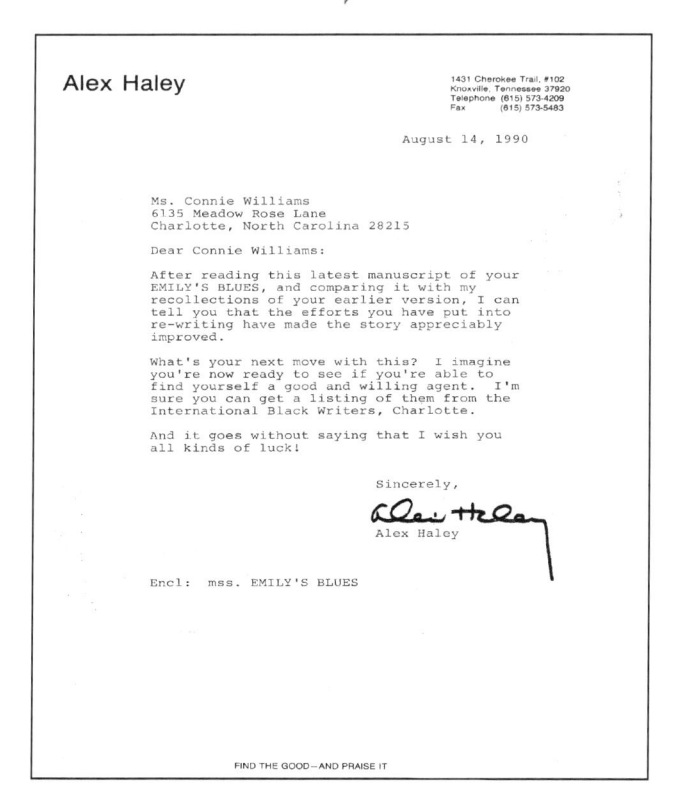

> **Alex Haley**
> 1431 Cherokee Trail, #102
> Knoxville, Tennessee 37920
> Telephone (615) 573-4209
> Fax (615) 573-5483
>
> August 14, 1990
>
> Ms. Connie Williams
> 6135 Meadow Rose Lane
> Charlotte, North Carolina 28215
>
> Dear Connie Williams:
>
> After reading this latest manuscript of your EMILY'S BLUES, and comparing it with my recollections of your earlier version, I can tell you that the efforts you have put into re-writing have made the story appreciably improved.
>
> What's your next move with this? I imagine you're now ready to see if you're able to find yourself a good and willing agent. I'm sure you can get a listing of them from the International Black Writers, Charlotte.
>
> And it goes without saying that I wish you all kinds of luck!
>
> Sincerely,
>
> Alex Haley
>
> Encl: mss. EMILY'S BLUES
>
> FIND THE GOOD—AND PRAISE IT

Alex Haley

Oct. 20 1990

Ms. Connie Williams
6135 Meadow Rose Lane
Charlotte, North Carolina 28215

Dear Connie Williams —

You certainly do exhibit the spirit it takes to make it!

Sincerely,

Alex Haley

FIND THE GOOD — AND PRAISE IT

> Alex Haley
>
> Post Office Box L
> Norris, Tennessee 378
>
> October 28, 1991
>
> Ms. Connie Williams
> % African American Cultural Center
> 401 North Myers Street
> Charlotte, NC 28218
>
> Dear Connie:
>
> Your letter lacks something vital, which so many letters do; a return address. Fortunately the flier which you sent contained the address of the Cultural Center which I am using.
>
> Principally, I just wanted to drop a quick note here in the middle of the night to say how much I enjoyed having the little note from some of your students and the letter from yourself and I want to wish you all kinds of luck with your work. You are doing what one has to do if one is to succeed: never quit!
>
> Yours sincerely,
>
> Alex Haley
>
> FIND THE GOOD—AND PRAISE IT

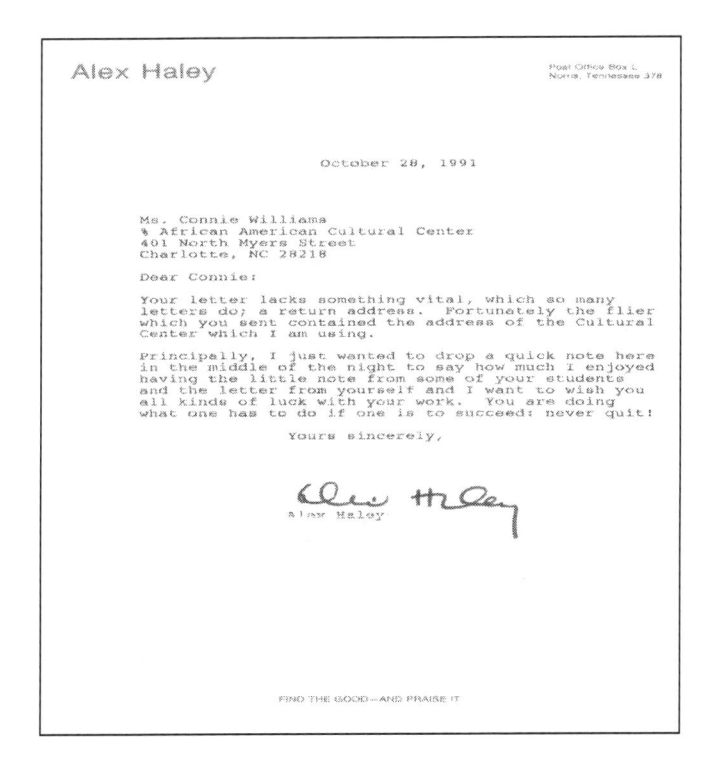

In his speech at the Writing Convention in 1990, the late Alex Haley said there are three important concepts about writing: 1). A writer should write about what is close with him/her. 2). Preserve the history. 3). Educate publishers on the market for the work—a need for the story, then cast a spell so the reader will never be able to get rid of it once it's in their head.

I have taken his advice to heart—they are words to live by as a writer.

I admired the way he felt about celebrity. Feb 12, 1992 **... Alex Haley** told friends, "I am just a **writer** trying to make a living."

While at Piedmont, my organization EBSAP sponsored the world renowned author of Clover, Dori Sanders, and the NFL football player (my cousin) Ethan Horton of the Los Angeles Raiders, both to speak to students.

Inasmuch as I enjoyed my position at Piedmont, as I became more mature, a decision occurred to me, when God laid it upon my heart, I answered his call to transfer from Union County Schools to Charlotte-Mecklenburg Schools to teach where I resided and eliminate the early morning drive from Charlotte to Monroe each morning. Some of those country curvy roads on a cold and snowy morning could be treacherous and hazardous.

Of course, my principal at Piedmont didn't want me to transfer, and I knew I would miss "my people." But I managed to bid them a farewell after many well-wishes and a lovely lunch.

The new school, the shorter driving distance and my new appointments as tenth grade English teacher/ tenth-grade chair and Mentoring of the new teachers in the English Department served to be both challenging and interesting.

Tenth graders were required to pass a writing test with a score of three or above. To help my students, I invited the parents of the students to the After-School Tutoring sessions. Most of my students passed their test with a score of three and fours, and one parent and I became and have remained friends over the years. In fact, she has been a constant influence for the readings and presentations of my books at the McCorey YMCA, First Baptist West Church, and Little Rock AME Zion Church.

God allowed me to teach for twelve years in the Charlotte-Mecklenburg School System. Unfortunately, I must admit, administration and politics have a way of forcing excellent teachers to leave the profession. When I retired from one of the high schools, I left partly because of a lack of respect I received from administration; lousy facilities that "any professional educator should have to encounter." After teaching in CMS for nine years, my classroom was relocated to a room that once served as the Home Economics classroom where old equipment was still in the back of the room that carried odors from what I believe were rodents. There was also a chained-up cabinet that I had to demand many times before it actually happened that the chains are cut off finally. They were cut off, but not without many requests and adamant rejections from a colleague who stored books there.

Additionally, it appeared that administration seemed to become annoyed when one solicited support personnel to remove unruly students from the classroom. Then the political policy was to use an "Action Plan" where the teacher had to "write up" post and submit copies to administration, an additional plan of action additional to what was already being used, as if the teacher had not already created, and made visible, the norms, procedures and consequences for students to follow in the classroom. This additional Action Plan still did not eliminate disruptive student behavior. Therefore the "Action Plan" it seemed was designed to literally "punish" the teacher for reprimanding the disruptive student who was obviously preventing other students from their Constitutional right to an education (Williams, 2015).

While God allowed my continued career in the Charlotte-Mecklenburg School system; I received the Master Teacher Bonus numerous years; my Teacher Observations were "Well Above Standard"; I received two Bright Idea Grants for innovative educational project; I once again introduced the world renowned author of *Clover*, Dori Sanders, to Charlotte-Mecklenburg Schools to discuss The Writing Process with students, and received a First Place Teamwork Award, and my name is included in the book *Who's Who Among American High School Teachers* for multiple years. I retired from CMS in 2006 while still teaching in the English Department at University of North Carolina at Charlotte until 2014.

God has been so good to me!

Chapter 13

∞

*A*s a result of God's inspiration to write *Emily's Blues,* I was also inspired to write a second letter of application to the Headlands Center for the Arts in Sausalito, California. My hope was to become a Writing Fellow. (My first letter of application to Headlands was not accepted). Following the second letter, the North Carolina Arts Council and the National Endowment for the Arts granted a Writing Fellowship for eight weeks, to Headlands. While I was there, learning my process; learning about installation art was a revelation. Reading in the hills of Tiburon, and getting acquainted with gallery crawls in San Francisco all related back to Washington and seeing Frederick Douglass's living room set up with the two desks.

    To become a Headlands Writing Fellow, God granted me the wisdom to write the following letter of application: the God-given courage to try again:

The letter: Headlands Center for the Arts
                  944 Fort Barry
Sausalito, California 94965

Dear Sir or Madam:

    In 1992, I was accepted as a Writing Fellow at the University of North Carolina at Charlotte. It was for me an experience that I shall never forget. The diversity of the aesthetic and cultural mix enabled me to view art's significance in an expanded gregarious, cultivation of knowledge.

    While at UNCC, I developed a collection of Haiku poetry, a one-act stage play, which was funded by the Union County Community Arts Council and performed at Piedmont High School by regular program and students with special needs where I teach. This one-act stage play won the Senator Terry Sanford NCAE Award for Creativity. I also began and later completed a second novel of fiction. I have wanted to continue this unique experience. It was at UNCC that I learned to use a Macintosh Computer and the Eric system. HEADLANDS laboratory for creativity will continue to stimulate this vision of light and grasp for new ideas.

I feel that, as an African American writer, I have a responsibility to help bring about an awareness of experiences of a certain criteria and caliber to our society in writing. I am particularly interested in the works of several writers and psychologists, among them are: Abraham Maslow, Maya Angelou and James Baldwin.

For the past year I have been performing public readings at schools and bookstores and developing three major manuscripts that are interrelated. I believe the residency at Headlands will provide exposure and experiences conducive to writing and research for innovative thoughts; therefore, I hope that I will be accepted into the center.

Very sincerely yours,
Connie Williams

Two years later, based on God's favor, and as a result of this second letter of application to Headlands, the director of the arts center flew from Sausalito to North Carolina to interview me in Raleigh, North Carolina, and her objective was to listen to a reading from my first novel, *Emily's Blues*. Later the North Carolina Arts Council and the National Endowment for the Arts sent me a Letter of Acceptance granting an eight-week Fellowship as a Headlands (AIR) Artist in Residence Fellow and a contract in 1996.

In June I boarded a plane to San Francisco, and a volunteer for Headlands, James V., met me at the airport and drove us across the Golden Gate Bridge to Maurin County to Headlands in his Porsche.

God is good. What He has in store
for you cannot be changed. God will put
you where He wants you to be even if
others do not think you deserve it.

At Headlands I was provided with my very own studio with a computer where I continued to work on the *Sequel* to *Emily's Blues* the manuscript that I began as a writing Fellow at UNCC, and I completed the first draft of a new novel, *Green*.

Little did I know that as a Headlands Center for the Arts Heir I would possibly collaborate with United States and international artists from all over the world: Sweden, Italy, Canada, India, Czech Republic, Germany, Croatia, Mexico, Taiwan, and Slovakia. (One of my photos is taken where I'm sitting on a sculpture by one of the international artists.

Connie Williams   This Life: Through
                                   Grace Hope and Mercy

Installation art created while at Headlands.

Connie Williams   This Life: Through Grace Hope and Mercy

Installation art "mixed images."

The above image includes a photo of me while at Headlands perched on a sculpture created by an international artist that is to be shipped to Germany.

Below is the **Headlands Journal written** while there to glorify what God has done for me—allowing experiences that others perhaps only dream about:

June 12: While riding to Headlands, James V. and I had a chance to talk. I learned that he is a Cardboard Display Designer for a computer company in San Francisco. He also teaches his craft to young students. And last year his fourteen-year-old nephew came to live with him for a year.

The Residency Manager Holly B. was to meet me in the am to take me to the bank and the grocery store. Before leaving with Holly, I met most of the Headland's big wigs: I saw the Executive Director who interviewed me again and the Program Director; Director of Operations; the Chef in the Mess Hall where many of us love to hang out. I also met the Public Relations Manager and the Executive Assistant.

I was given the keys and James V. a lovely person, too bad he's not about ten years older or I'm not BLANK years younger. Anyway, James helped me take my bags to my art studio where I would be working and staying—a spacious room on the second floor at Building 940.

LaVerne Z., a writer from Kentucky, whom I also had met earlier, whose studio was also in my building; her door was open and I could see that she was sitting and working at her computer on an art project and interested in talking; she told me "Bridging the gap on how to articulate what she does as an artist to the community." As she elaborated further, I thought to myself, I do something like this myself: Serving those individuals that have been previously underserved and trying to find a way to explain the need for art involvement on a larger scale, i.e. Art in social studies; art in Science I remember the question being asked of me, "Why would you need to teach art? You teach English. Well I responded, "English is literature; literature is art."

LaVerne Z. – Kentucky questions Friday and Saturday eating arrangements (eat on your own—Fir and Sat).

Salad at dinner the first night: Cabbage, tomatoes, peanuts chili, picked tea leaves, fried garlic, shredded ginger oil, peanut oil, salt, lemon Lehpet means tea salad. Burmese tea leaves with Drake (duck).

Later that evening I had my first meal at the dining table in the Mess Hall located in the main building. Thet S. W. from the Bay Area (San Francisco Bay), made her famous Lehpet Dake Salad; it means: Tea Salad from Burma. It consisted of cabbage, tomatoes, peanuts chili, pickled tea leaves, fried garlic, shredded ginger, peanut oil, salt and lemon. I thought, very tasty indeed.

At dinner I also met Irene S. a painter from Chapel Hill, North Carolina and Jimmy T., from Austin, TX a dancer who combines elements of American Sign Language and African dance ritual. Jimmy is a former member of the National Theater of the Deaf and an incredibly intelligent person. Michal G. and his wife and three children from Czech Republic, also included were Henrik H. an installation artist and his girlfriend Lotta from Sweden and Franz J. also an installation artist from Germany was included.

June 13, 1996: Thursday, up at 7:30 a.m. met Sharon at the house next to 940. She's from San Francisco and on a week's stay here. We exchanged names and some information about a Charlotte artist Aalonjo D. She may come back to Open House on July 21 here at the center. I gave her a business card.

Mel C. a sculptor and installation/conceptual artist arrived to help fill sandbags with sand to help with the Landscape Project (the new parking lot), to take place on Sunday.

I'm waiting now for Holly; she's supposed to be here at 9:30 a.m. to take me shopping in Sausalito for the first time since my arrival. My check was in my mailbox. I signed up to take the center car next weekend, Friday and Saturday, to go sightseeing.

Holly arrived around ten o'clock. We took her truck into the city of Sausalito to bank and to grocery shop at Molly Stones, a gourmet grocery and glitzy supermarket where everyone just loves the produce, including me. As she glided over the hills and around the curves of Bridge Way, 101 and Blithway, I had a chance to see some of the landscape on the way to bank at West America Bank.

I spent $50.00 on some chicken soup, bread, juice Hummus, cheap wine (6.79) avocados, crackers, Zip lock freezer bags, grapefruit juice, and a 99-cent jug of water, peppermint tea, and sharp cheddar cheese and flower Tortilla.

Returned to the house – Holly helped me bring up the groceries while we chatted about the prices of food, other artists, my studio and my work, and she soon left to get back to the main house to work. I know we had decided last night during dinner that we would attend an art exhibit in San Rafael at five. I wrote for a short while on the computer and drank some green tea which made my eyelids too heavy to keep them open and I had to have a short nap. I was exhausted. Traveling across three time zones I'm sure jet lag still had its effects on me.

I woke up around four-thirty seeing that it was too early to dress for the trip to the gallery; I took a walk down to check my mail – read the San Francisco newspaper about the big celebration to take place on Friday to honor this some special person and Walter Cronkite was to attend. I talked briefly to Katherine, B, one of the center's administrators, who was in the kitchen with Lori, I believe getting some lunch (he's really cute--nice body, and seems nice—kind face—approachable). It makes a man almost absolutely irresistible when he's good looking, and polite. Anyway, I sat out in the shade on the porch near the kitchen where Donna and Heather who work at the center sat discussing art-center shop. Katherine came out with people she was meeting for lunch, to whom she readily introduced me. We exchanged the usual information about each other—where are you from etc. I told them and asked the same of them etc. Then after a while growing tired of shop talk, I excused myself and decided to take a short walk going up the road pass the two large artist houses next to the house with my studio it being an unusually beautiful day. I was tempted to visit Loraine but then my stomach reminded me that I needed to get a little something to eat before going to the exhibit later and time was fleeting. I returned to my studio and prepared some Cream of Chicken soup in the kitchen. While I sat there eating, LaVerne came in and said she was about to dress for our trip. She left the kitchen to go into her studio, which is located next door to mine.

I yelled to her, "Are you dressing up?"

She returned, "No, I'm just going to change my jeans."

"All I need to do is get a jacket because I don't want to be cold later. I felt an ache in my right ear when I got up this morning. I must have gotten a chill during the night."

"I'm wearing a heavy sweater. Are you changing clothes?" LaVerne yelled!

"No, I put on a fresh pair of jeans this morning so I don't think I need to." I answered.

I finished my soup, cleaned up what I messed up in the kitchen and went into my studio to put another shirt underneath the one I was wearing. I put on some lipstick. By now LaVerne was yelling, "I'm going downstairs to the bathroom and then I'll be ready." I yelled back, "Okay."

I met LaVerne downstairs and we left the house, walked down to 944 to the kitchen where Michael waited with his wife and three children. I met Martin P. an attorney from the Bay area. Irene S. came in and said she would need to change her shorts. She and Thet S. W. had been at the beach. There was some discussion about how many cars would need to be driven and we learned that Michael would drive one of the center's cars. Martin said everybody was welcome to go in his 1956 Chevy. Martin, and LaVerne jumped into the front seat of his Chevy. He stopped to pick up Irene and Thet down the road. When they climbed into the back seat, I began to feel a little chilly so I asked Thet to loan me a scarf since we were close to her studio. I felt she could run in and out again. She got out of the car disappeared for a moment and then returned with a huge black scarf and reached her hand over the back seat to hand it to me with a gigantic smile across her moon-oriental soft-looking olive face. I reciprocated her smile, accepted the scarf from her hand and instantly began rapping it around my neck. Everyone wanted to know if I felt better, and I assured them that I indeed did feel warmer.

We took off through the one-way tunnel toward Highway 101 with Martin behind the wheel on our way to the gallery crawl in the curvy, steep hills in San Francisco. I'm thinking to myself; I love this car. On the way there was this incredible discussion about LaVerne Z.'s Community Based Writing program, and if a "sequence trail" is better than a "paper trail" etc.

****

I was given direction on how to get around in Mill Valley, so I gathered up my courage to sign out a Headlands car: Car tag 2PGY906. Rosenstock: Directions: See stop. See horses on a two-way highway- heading east toward Sausalito. (Go west and you end up running out of land). Come to another stop sign see housing of the old Fort. Take the tunnel – (one-way tunnel) out of the tunnel fort Barry, make a left to Alexander Avenue. See the Bay (Alcolrant) to the right - Hills and houses continue curving around right on Harbor drive left to West America Bank. Take Bridgeway and Harbor Drive – take 101 north to Strawberry Village to Safeway grocery store.

Back to Headlands for dinner. Everyone including Franz John and his family—wife and three children from Germany. Saw Franz's wood-carved sculpture today that will be shipped to Germany. After dinner, Irene S, Thet S and Martin P and I went into San Francisco to North Beach to see a movie "Welcome to the Doll House." We took the scenic route over the Golden Gate Bridge. Back to my studio at midnight. I later showed the movie to my Garinger High School students once back in North Carolina.

June 14, 1996: Friday. Shampooed my hair, ate breakfast, talked to Laverne and Jimmy who's deaf and a creative dancer whose studio is down stairs and his friend while eating breakfast in the kitchen. I went down to 944 to get a computer for my studio. Holly brought her truck around loaded it on to the back and then carried it up to my studio. We set it up and I plugged it in and clicked onto Headlands Center for the Arts icon applications Mac Word. Mac files I. Connie Williams – Biography. 2. Sequel. I'm ready to rock and roll.

June 15, l996: Saturday: Morning 6:30 a.m. Ate breakfast—Jewish rye with cheese, avocado and Hummus, grapefruit juice and water. I Wrote out Thursday's memoirs, afterwards—decided to rearrange my studio—moving the bed, the rug, the desk and the TV—Then worked on my biography.

Workshop at 944 with Lavern Z., Will P. and Genn L. called "Everybody's write": A workshop on Community Based Writing. The three components were: Panel discussion; Writing exercise and Informal discussion group.

June 16, 1996:

A famous person once said with the proper funding—agents, publishing houses willing to give a chance, there could have perhaps been another Muddy Waters.

Called my father and my brother for Father's Day and called a significant other in North Carolina too. Worked on my novel and later went down to 944 for the Big BBQ Lori had prepared for the Landscape Project. Great food and great day!

June 17, 1996

Rhea L. a teacher of theater at the University of Lexington, KY, Lavern and I went to Sausalito to shop. As we rounded the curve to go into the tunnel, we caught a glimpse of Jimmy Turner rollerblading. Later, Holly called and told us that Lori the chef was sick and that we were to eat the leftovers from the BBQ.

June 18, 1996

Wrote chapter two of my new novel. At just about the time that I needed a break, Laverne knocked on my door wanting to know if I wanted to paint with her and Rhea.

They had spread paint with brushes and paper on the kitchen table—we must have spent three hours just fooling around with creating some design on paper for greeting cards.

June 19, 1996

I wrote chapter three of my new novel. Made some changes to chapter one of the novel. Later at dinner (Wednesday night) the Headlands Board members came and introduced themselves. After dinner Rhea, Laverne and I went walking over the Golden Gate Bridge and took some photos. When we arrived back to 940, our studio house, Jimmy was in the kitchen with two friends laughing it up and using sign language.

June 20, 1996

It was Summer-Salon-Swedish-party night. A table was set up in the grass for dinner to celebrate Swedish Harvest with herring, boiled potatoes, green salad, cheese, buttered bread, pickled beets and plenty of Vodka, beer and wine, which we drank after a song that I don't quite remember except for the first line, that may have been Skal, a Swedish term for, (down the hatch or cheers) said right before having a shot of alcohol.

June 21, 1996

I had the car signed out, and dropped LaVerne and Rhea off to take the Ferry to San Francisco, and I just drove around Marin, located in the San Francisco Bay Area, and walked around leisurely all day and shopped.

June 22, 1996.

My brother, Don, friend Wilma, and significant other called. I returned them all. I had the car signed out; drove to Sausalito. Later there was a party at

Thet and Irene's house for the Czech family who were leaving and returning to Germany.

Irene has a tape that she said she will tape for me by Sly and the Family Stones that I haven't heard since I gave it away when I moved to North Carolina. James was at the party, and we began talking and I told him about an idea that I am trying to put together concerning motivating fourth graders to write an ending to a story, and incorporate the use of the computer program and visual art. We discussed it and then included Irene into the plan with visual art. We agreed to meet on Tuesday to discuss this further.

June 23, 1996

Called my family and talked to my brother Don (he was keeping my car at his house). Everyone is fine on the home front. I worked on the novel and this journal.

June 24, 1996

I took Laverne and Rhea into Sausalito to catch the Ferry to San Fernando to go shopping. Coming home there was an accident on the Golden Gate and traffic was backed up for at least a mile and a half, and therefore, it caused me to be stuck in traffic for almost three hours from 4:45 p.m. until 7:00 p.m. Arrived back at the Center and wrote on the novel before dinner.

June 25, 1996

I met with James and Irene at the main Building 944, at ten o'clock to continue plans for the Beasley Story Writing. I met the new artist from Ohio, David S., a writer and professor of English at Tiffin University, and a newspaper journalist.

June 26, 1996

I wrote chapter four to the new novel, and later I met the new artist, Katherine B. from Minneapolis, MN an intern from Harvard majoring in English and Fine Art. At dinner I met Gretchen C., a sculptor and her husband, Malcolm C. a sculptor/installation artist both from Columbus, Ohio. They had their children with then, Willa and Nora. Lavern's eleven years old son Johnny arrived from KY.

June 27, 1996

Made changes to the novel. Went down to the Mess Hall and Lori was running late with dinner. We all pitched in to help her make dinner using an Indian recipe with flat bread, lots of beer and wine on the table.

June 28, 1996

Frizie drove us into Sausalito to catch the Golden Gate Ferry to San Francisco. Laverne, her son Johnny and I went to the Island Alcatraz, then to Chinatown, the Haines Gallery and Barnes and Noble Books. Johnny bought Dennis Rodman's book, *BAD AS I WANT TO BE*.

When we return to the Center, I had missed James' call that came in around 10: a.m. with more information about the BEASLEY PROJECT.

June 29, 1996

I was invited to go out to Mill Valley and surf with Johnny and LaVerne, but I needed to stay and catch up on my writing. I telephoned my children: talked to them. I wrote my parents and my oldest sister Pat in NC, telephoned James again and left a message. He returned my call around three. We discussed the 'B' Project and made plans to have a mini meeting tomorrow at the MATTERS OF FAITH Spiritual Exploration.

Although I'm here among the hills the trees the ocean and of course the awesome bridge, the real beauty of it all is the people—the gregarious yet diverse cultural mix: The coming together, the sharing of ideas, the blending of events in something that seems as simple as helping Lori the chef in the Mess Hall that has the potential of turning into a grand time of storytelling and laughter—the willingness to converse and share. I don't believe that I've ever seen anything like it. Although I was a Writing Fellow at UNC at Charlotte where similar components and events happened, perhaps the differences are geographic—mountains, water and the sweetness of freedom of time and choice.

June 30, 1996

Matter of Faith: A Spiritual Exploration of Place and Community with Linda Tillery and the Cultural Heritage Choirs, Wendy Johnson Buddhism's at Zen Center's Green Gulch Farm in Marin County; Lois Lurentzen professor of social ethics at University of San Francisco specializes in environmental ethics; L. Frank Manriquez, Tongva/Ajachmem, painter and sculptor who documented Native American artifacts in Paris' Muse de L'Homme; Victor Pereira a journalist and teacher at U.C Berkeley; Victoria Rue, feminist theologian, playwright, director and holds a PhD in Theology and Jimmy Turner, a former member of the National Theater of the Deaf. What an invigorating day; the discussions were inspiring and transforming.

July 1, 1996

I worked on the 'Beasley' Storytelling Project and the Journal. I went down to the main building to pick up the key and met the new artist, Barbara H. who once lived in San Francisco and now lives in New York. Took the car and went into Sausalito to run my errands, bank, develop some film, Molly Stone's grocery store and window shop. I tried to find the library to research Brunswick stew (for when I may prepare a meal for Carolina night), but was unsuccessful. Came home and worked on the novel.

Went down to dinner at six o'clock and Lori was running a little late and needed some eggs to bake cookies. I thought Thet might have some so I ran up to her studio and she called Katherine and she did have some. In the meanwhile, while I was in her studio, Thet showed me her projects and I shared with her that my father was in upholstery. She said great because she was upholstering buttons with a beautiful red material and we covered some buttons together before going to dinner.

Dinner was Mexican night with the whole enchiladas, we talked of it being Jimmy's last night and we were all going on a moonlight hike. It was very foggy outside and beginning to get chilly. After dinner, I went up to my studio to get a sweater and a scarf for the walk. While waiting to go on the hike, my friend called from North Carolina.

Afterwards, just as I opened the door to leave the studio for the hike, Jimmy was crawling up the hill in front of the house. I couldn't tell if he was an animal or human at first. Then he shined his flashlight on me and we both burst into a big laugh. Jimmy and I walked arm in arm back down to the kitchen where everyone waited outside.

Malcolm was there in the van with his wife and two daughters. I rode with them down to the beach. The others rode on the back of Thet's truck.

At the beach we hopped out of the van and hiked up a very steep trail to the top of one of the hills and Jimmy wanted us to form a circle. Then he lit some sage, and gave each of us a piece to rub in our hands and to keep it. He signed and the interpreter told us what he was saying. "Take a deep breath and that whenever he sees the stars, the moon, the water and the trees, he will remember us." He signed, "I love you all and will miss you." He then moved around from the circle and hugged each one of us: Malcolm, Grechen, Lotta, Henrik, Willa and Nora, Lori, Franz, Thet, Katherine and me.

We returned to the automobiles by way of a very narrow and steep hill, and then each to our own studios. Before going to bed, I arranged with LaVerne to have Johnny participate in the testing of the 'Beasley' Project.

July 2, 1996

Up at seven-thirty a.m. to get the business meeting organized. I telephoned Irene and left a message that we could go to James' house to work out the bugs in the 'B' Project. I called James at nine a.m. Went down and arranged for transportation to Mill Valley where the meeting was to take place. Irene and I jumped into the car and took off for James's around noon. James showed us the Painter Computer Program and the HyperCard Program. We also discussed the objectives and the layout for the project. We returned to our studios around four o'clock in the afternoon. Looked over Johnny's responses to the project, he had created a short story. I also worked with him on getting a model to start his visual image of a dog. Worked on the novel. I'm up to chapter five. Went to dinner at six thirty. Came home feeling really exhausted. Took a shower and went to bed.

July 3, 1996

At nine a.m. I heard a knock at the door and it was Johnny, LaVerne's eleven-year-old son who was about to leave and return to Kentucky. He was coming to say good bye. We hugged a very big and long hug, and I walked with him over to his mom's studio. We chatted and then the two of them left for the San Francisco Airport.

I later ate breakfast and dressed and spent the rest of the day working on the novel, the project and the journal and getting prepared for Show and Tell taking place that evening at the main building.

At Show and Tell all live-in AIRs (Artist in Residence) as well as Affiliate Artists and those who did not show in April with last names from K to Z presented, slides, readings, videos, etc. for approximately ten minutes or talk about their work. Guests were present and dinner was served to all. Guest dinners cost six dollars a person. The new artist Adam B., Installations artist came in from Toronto, Canada. I performed a reading from my work in progress, *GREEN*, many slides were taken of my reading presentation.

July 4, 1996

Headland's is closed to the public today since it is a holiday. I started my regular routine: exercise program again this morning. During the early hours, I worked on the Journal, the novel. Later a group of us will get together for Pot Luck dinner and then go up the hill at the beach to watch the fireworks. San Francisco and Sausalito will be too crowded to go there with the tourist, parades and all. And besides, my skin is beginning to get a little irritated by the hot sun.

We all climbed into cars and headed up the hill and across the Golden Gate Bridge to see fireworks from San Francisco.

July 5, 1996

Had the car signed out; went to the post office, the bank, Calendonia Library to get some information from the LMP and to do some research for Malcolm C. Came home at five; worked on the novel. Later I began to experiment with the camera and photo layouts, installations. Took four photos of my instillations and was anxious to see the installation outcome.

Installation Art: July 6, 1996

    Today we went to Mill Valley and shopped. I had the experiment photos devolped and started looking at them in the car on the way home. They came out better than I expected. Returned and prepred dinner, boiled corn on the cob, salad with avacodo and cheese with buttermilk ranch dressing, spaghetti noodles with cheese and black olives and toasted bagle; plain pound cake and peppermint tea—I ate. After dinner, I worked on the Journal and the novel. Up to chapter six. Thank you Lord

July 7 and 8, 1996: Worked on *Green*.

July 9, 1996

Worked on *Sequel* to *Emily's Blues*

July 10 through 14, 1996 Physical workout each a.m.

July 15, l996: Saturday: Morning 6:30 a.m. Ate breakfast—Jewish rye with cheese, avocado and Hummus, grapefruit juice and water. I wrote out Thursday's memoirs. I decided to rearrange my studio—moved the bed, the rug, the desk and the TV. I worked on my biography/ Physical workout.

July 16, 1996:

Left Headlands Center with LaVerne and she drove me across the Golden Gate Bridge into San Francisco to take the Grayhound bus to Los Angeles to visit my family, Pricillia and her husband Clint who lives in the San Fernando Valley. Mrs. Stamps, my daughter's mother-in-law and her son, Clint Sr., drove to Los Angeles from the Valley to pick me up at the bus station and then drove me to Lake View to see my daughter and my grandchildren. We stayed up all night talking, catching up, taking photos and bonding. I stayed two nights there and then rented a car; took the 118 Freeway into Northridge my alma mater at California State University Northridge. I rode around the west valley site seeing and shopping, bought two rayon and cotton dresses—great finds.

I had to be in Los Angeles at two o'clock to pick up my friend and school chum Wilma at the main Post Office where she works in the Investigative Division. After visiting at her job and meeting some of her colleagues, the two of us left Los Angeles and drove to Ontario where she resides. We had dinner and went out to a movie with her friend.

My California Sister in Christ

On Saturday, Wilma and I did the "girlfriend thing" — went out shopping, then returned the rental car and ate pancakes, bacon and eggs for breakfast at the Kuntry Kitchen. Later that day, her sister Verna came over driving her Cadillac, with it's plush leather seats. She took us to Ontario Mills Mall for more shopping, where I purchased a purple and white summer jumpsuit to wear to barbecue outings. This mall happens to be the largest shopping **mall** in San Bernardino County, California. It is located in **Ontario, California**, and with 28 million annual visitors, so to say the very least it was extremely crowded. But it was an enjoyable venture.

Once again while we sat around bonding, my X-sister-in-law Lizzie showed up for a visit to see us, which we all were so happy to see her, and I felt was such a thouthtful thing of her to keep in touch. Lizzie lives in the Valley too; transitioned to California right after graduating from high school. And back then I didn't think she'd looked back even once to consider returning to North Carolina. Now, I believe this has changed. I hear she might be planning to relocate. I do see her from time to time at our annual Winchester school reunion.

At ten o'clock that night, Wilma drove me from Ontario to Clairmont so I could take the Greyhound back to Los Angeles and then on to San

Francisco where LaVern, an artist from Headlands, would pick me up there, and we would drive over the Golden Gate back to Headlands Center on Sunday.

I made the ride to Los Angeles, but the bus ride to San Francisco almost didn't happen because one of the attendants at the station informed me that the bus was full; there were no more seats and that it would be necessary for me to wait until the following day to return to San Francisco.

But I informed the attendant, "I am an Artist in Residence at Headlands Center for the Arts in Sausalito, California, and it is manditory that I leave tonight."

The attendant informed me, "I'll see what we can do." And within a matter of an hour or less, I was told by a kindly, gray-haired gentlemen, "We have managed to provide a seat for you on the next bus going to San Francisco. Come with me to purchase your ticket."

I followed him to the ticket window and handed over the money to the attendant.

The Greyhound bus pulled out of the station around one in the A.M., and I made the eight and a half hour overnight trip back to San Francisco. At close to 12 noon the weather was fine; I purchased a cup of coffee and pack of peanut butter crackers from the vending machine. Lavern was coming at one so I decided to wait outside in the open air because the station was very crowded. And earlier inside before purchasing my snack, I sat down and a very long-haired nomad, dressed in soiled ragged clothes sat directly beside me. I didn't pay it much attention until he crossed one leg over the other and I noticed his dirty socks sticking out of the toe of his shoe, and I suddenly sucked in some pungent foul odor that went directly into and seemed to burn the inside of my nostrils.

So I eased out of my seat; went outside to wait for Lavern who drove up with a big "Hello" right on schedule in front of the Greyhound Bus Station in San Francisco.

Back at Headlands, at seven-thirty we had dinner with everyone at the Center. It was Bastile Day and a French dinner had been prepared. Willa and Nora, Grechen and Malcolm's daughters wanted to read chapter one of my new novel. When they finished reading, we discussed what they liked about it and what stuck in their minds. I received great reviews from the both of the daughters. Now they want to read chapter two. I told them "I'll think about it." Later, I decided not to allow them to read it.

Retrospectfully, now I wished I had. What could it have hurt—nothing!

My endeavor was to try and maximum my time and catch up on the writing of the new novel since I had been away seeing my family.

> The Lord knew my heart and allowed
> me to pour out words on the computer.
> Thank you Lord for your favor. (Getting
> what God has for you. Nothing can block
> God's plan. But you must stay on the
> course to receive what He has. If you
> stray, you change the plan. You go through
> the storm to get to the rainbow.
> Preparation determines your destination.
> God establish Joshua as His representative
> to guide the nation the Red Sea in front of
> them and Pharaoh and his chariots behind
> them. Joshua represented a new vision from
> Egypt across the Red Sea from devastation to
> liberation to ownership. God said you got to
> believe me and I'll show you). (Joshua 3:1-4:24)

July 17, 1996

We had dinner the usual time at dining room and it was Salon night. Bretta C. from Germany presented her installation art work. Whe talked of the sewing factory (sweat shops) and there was a drawing which she created that reminded me of the days I worked at Allen Overall in North Carolina making Army jackets for the military. She reminded me too of Mama's sewing machine which was one of her prize possessions—Mama could create and make anything on her old pedal driven Sears Sewing Machine.

I returned to the studio to work some more on the novel. I was still tired from the trip. Along about twelve midnight, the lines of a poem started to come to my head and I couldn't sleep, so I got up and wrote "Headlands Lovesong." At four in the morning I finally climbed into bed able to sleep.

July 18, 1996

Rode into Mill Valley to shop and go to the bank with LaVerne. Returned to the studio and worked on chapter 8 the final chapter of the Sequel. After dinner I allowed Nora to read the new poem.

A luncheon and workshop was held in Tiburan, CA at one of the board members I'Lea's house, and Donna from the office invited me to attend. It was up in the hills in this beautiful home surrounded with a garden, swimming pool and a view over looking the ocean. It was incredible. I recently learned that Robin Williams lived and died in Tiburan in 2014.

Situated on the patio were five tables with the most elegant lunch settings. A maid served us and all the ladies were very mature and professional, like designers, writers, publishers, business women etc. Headlands Center For the Arts director did her introduction and we all introduced ourselves. They asked me to read one of my poems. I was happy to persent. Afterwards, we completed a writing activity and ate lunch.

Laverne asked me to read my new poem, "Headlands Lovesong," which was received well.

Later I managed to get so many contacts, information for publishers, bookstores that would carry my novel. At dinner I'Lea came up and asked me what the book was about and that she was the owner of Depot Books and would carry it in her Mill Valley store once it's complete.

James V. came up and said we should meet tomorrow to complete the work on the 'B' Project. I also got a chance to talk to Opel P. Adisa, a writer and Ph.D from Jamaica. In a long and delightful talk, she shared some information about publishers.

July 19, 1996

At breakfast had a talk with LaVerne. I think we both awoke with a cataclysmic question on focus and life sequences involving our work from this point in time on, and our transformation as artists. I wrote a new poem, "Hands," dedicated to Daddy. I continued working on chapter 8 of the novel. Met with James at five o'clock to work on the 'B'Project.

July 20, 1996

Met with James to work on the 'B' Project.

July 21, 1996

Open House and my first public reading of chapter one of *GREEN*. Lori our chef's boyfriend died while in Brum (Birmingham, England), therefore we had to "fend" for ourselves for meals in the kitchen. Lori went to England for the memorial.

July 23, 1996

Completed first draft of the third novel, *EMILY'S SEQUEL*. At dinner all the artists drank to my success. Later the writers' held open house and all the artists came to our studios for readings and persentations. I read from *GREEN*.

July 24, 1996

Barbara H. a film artist showed her film, "Tender Fictions" in the East Wing. Met Ken and talked to him about writing a screen play.

July 25, 1996

Met with Erin B. at 11:30 a.m., she came up to my studio, and we sat around talking about writing and publishing. She also has a novel in progress. We made a business agreement that she will edit my manuscript for hire at a reasonable price.

LaVerne left today. Before leaving we had a talk and her advise to me was:

"Connie you have a lot of space—but if you let someone come into your life, be careful. He will have to have himself together, or he'll come in and suck that space right out of your head. They're not going to take it out of your classroom, nor out of your house. They're going to take it right out of your head. So they really have to have themselves together—so be careful and keep on being selective."

I wrote my professional resume and completed the typing, editing and printing. I ate dinner and went to Katherine R's. home to watch a movie, "The Field" with other artists.

I Picked up the Evaluation of Artist-In-Residence Program questions today from my mailbox. Holly asked to schedule my Exit Interview on Thrusday at either eleven or one o'clock. My exit interview went very well.

On the evening before I was to leave the next day, an artist, Mario, from Mexico arrive that morning. He drove me in a Headlands car to Mill Valley to gas the car for the trip over the bridge to San Francisco where I would take a plane to North Carolina. On the way from Mill Valley, there were rabbits, deer, and raccoons running through the hills and over the trails. Mario said, "Connie, all the animals have come out to say good-bye to you."

God laid these words on my heart to write the evaluation: Evaluation Letter to: The Grants Office, North Carolina Arts Council, Department of Cultural Resources, Raleigh, North Carolina, 27601-2807.

Dear Sir or Madam: This report serves to catalogue the highlights of the Headlands Center for the Arts Residency for June 12, 1996 through August 7, 1996 in Sausalito California.

The North Carolina Arts Council, The National Endownment for the Arts and Headlands Center for the Arts have provided an enlightening, transformational and cultural experience for artistic growth and development through the two-month residency.

Headlands carries out its mission by providing a catalyst for creative thinking and problem solving. As an artist I found that the location, the divesity of the aesthetic and cultural mix, the work/live space and the allotted time enhanced the creative flow of energy enabling me to view art's significance in a continuous gregarious, cultivation of knowledge. The forming of partnerships was smooth and enthusiastic. Communities became camaraderies where schools of thought were discussed and analyzed, ideas were shared and accepted. There were numerous opportunities to explore and experiment with new ideas and practices which were encouraged. I wrote the first draft of my third novel, collaborated with two other artists on a major Children's Storytelling Project. I experimented with original art sketches on pages of poetry written at Headlands and made a delightful discovery. As an artist, (a writer) I discovered that my work is more visual than I realized.

Headlands experience was transformational. My focus is much clearer than when I arrived. I learned that as an artist, I AM APPRECIATED FOR MY WORK. This is an excellent way to exemplify support, respect and encouragement. The staff members were always available to assist in any way they could to help the artist carry out a goal, idea or solve a situation.

Linkage of the artists to the public and community is also a Headland's mission that serves to benefit a diverse group. I was invited to a luncheon in Tiberan sponsored by a Headlands Board member where I was given the opportunity to read my original poetry. Within this community, there were unique opportunities to converse and share some life as well as professional work experiences and establish ties for which the outcome may not manifest until a later time in my life.

The grounds at Headlands are magnificent. What a place for retreat and work. There are fond memories of the beaches, the ocean, the trails where foxes, raccoons and deer roam freely, where a group of us took a Moonlight Walk to say good-bye to a deaf dancer, Jimmy T., from Texas.

This report/evaluation would not be complete without some mention of the kitchen and Mess Hall facilities, which is a central gathering place that has been transformed by artist, Ann H. Lori M. is the chef whose meals include menus from around the world. Many events such as meetings, receptions and workshops took place in the kitchen. In the kitchen, I met artists from around the world, community people, Headlands Board members, dinner guests and established ties with people whom I personally and perfessionally plan to stay in touch.

A list of accomplishments while at Headlands follows: The first draft of a third novel of fiction entitled, Emily's Sequel; An extensive journal; three new poems—one includes art sketches; Collaboration with a visual artist and a cardboard display designer to create a computer story-telling program using an original children's story, "Miss Beasley and Miss Williams"; Reading at Show and Tell from a work in progress entitled, Green; Reading at Open House from Green; Experimention with instllation art, 'a photo collage'; Creation of a map and calling log; I began the first draft of a fourth novel (which later becomes the fifth novel of fiction), entitled, *QAK QAK*. Sincerely, Connie Williams;   cc/CW; Enclo

Chapter 14

∞

Giving God all the Honor and all of the Praise,

the contracts bearing my name that Alex Haley spoke of, they did manifest in many different forms after working long and hard over a considerable period and time: The Literary Circular Magazine, Editor Curtis Chisholm published *Emily's Blues* excerpt; A Sun Filled Dream, a book of poetry published two of my poems: Hands and Morn. And for the ones I'm most proud: Novello Festival Press of Charlotte, North Carolina, Editor Amy Rogers and the contract from the North

Carolina Arts Council for the Fellowship at Headlands Center for the Arts in Sausalito, CA. Novello finally accepted my short story "Mama Allie's Talking Dogs Fried Croakers in Peanut Oil, published in their food book of recipes and stories by writers around the North and South Carolinas, *Hungry For Home* in 2003. My first submission was a short story about an animal wanting chicken and dumplings; it was rejected because the editor stated they had many chicken and dumplings recipes and stories, so I quickly submitted "Mama Allie's 'talking dogs' Fried Croakers in Peanut Oil" recipe and it was quickly accepted.

> Show thy self worthy. Do all you can to present yourself to God as someone **worthy** of his approval. (Timothy 2:15)

From: NovelloFoodBook@aol.com
To: connie.williams@cms.k12.nc.us
Subject story

Hi Connie, I got your story and I think it will work fine—although it's a bit too long for the space and I will need to tighten it up a bit.

Is there a way you can send it to me via email so I don't have to retype it? You can send it as a Word attachment, or else cut and paste the text into an email message. Please let me know, either way.

Anything to save time really helps at this point! Thanks!

Amy Rogers, Executive Editor
Novello festival Press
___N. Tryon St., Charlotte, NC 28202
704-432-----
www.novellopress.org

I sometimes wonder if Novello knew just how important this email of acceptance of my work from them meant to me—it meant the world. Only a writer knows the work that actually goes into completing a story and getting it accepted by a publisher. Writing can be a lonely and sometimes disappointing process if you're doing it for the wrong reasons. I believe writers are chosen; writers must love the craft. As I write more and more, I know for sure that writing chose me.

> I believe that God chose me for this mission in life. God will place you where He wants you to be.

Alex Haley's advice of 'going from scratch to becoming a brain surgeon' has become more and more insightful.

Oftentimes when aspiring writers come to me for help, it is so difficult to get this point across to them just how many hours of hard work this process requires. Very seldom I turn them down. I sometimes feel bad for those I advise because I think they don't believe me when I give them the truth about the level of difficulty, and the truth is the best favor I can do for them.

****

Today, I cannot help but be overwhelmingly amazed at how God saved my life then and now He continually makes so many, many miracles from day by day for events that most overlook.

Some days I am mystified at people's immorality /falseness. I am perplexed at the inability to keep it real and tell the truth, for truth's sake. I know one thing for sure, is that I am NOT a perfect person. I know I make mistakes. I recall my Pastor saying, it is the hardest thing to try to do the right thing all the time. Considering that idea, I suppose when in matters of truth telling, it can possible be a difficult thing especially for those not in the habit of being trustworthy.

A case in point--For example, I have always been amazed at how writers advertise on the Web. I know I do have some advanced computer skills. I've taken numerous Computer courses at various workshops and universities. As a writer myself, I was often asked, do you have a Web Page? And now, with a lot of prayer and determination, today I do. So, one miracle is my Web page that reads:

[Connie Williams, Author of novels, *Green* and *Emily's Blues*. Connie Williams is a local author from North

Carolina, and California, the second of eleven children. Her parents, the late Jones and Lillie Williams were in the upholstery business and "fixed" most of the furniture in the town including the school superintendent's. Williams attributes her creativity to her parents. A writer and author of two novels: *Emily's Blues* republished in 2016 which originally made front page news in the Union Observer with its first publication. It was because of *Emily's Blues* that she became a Writer in Residence at Headlands Center for the Arts in Sausalito, California. It tells the story of how a teenage divorcee, and mother of four children, goes from poverty to a professional. Green tells the story of a young girl growing up and witnessing history in a small town during the civil rights era. Williams offers the experience of growing up in the rural South and details a young girl's life witnessing firsthand episodes of KKK threats in her hometown as she searches for her own identity. Both books: *Green* and *Emily's Blues* are available at Barnes and Noble; Amazon Books; Get Textbooks.com and Good Reads.com. Emily's Blues is also available on Amazon Kindle and several different countries].

I can recall in 2012, perhaps 2010 I was in need of help to set up and maintain some computer technology because I was embarking upon the process of putting together my new manuscript. Although I was constantly learning the skills, taking the workshops needed to teach multimodles and Portfolio where I taught English Composition and Inquiry at the University of North Carolina in the

English department, I still needed a computer technologist to help set up my desk-top publication, my Web page and Blog. Consequently, I reached out to one of my church members, a youthful male who was also employed at one of the colleges with whose family I'm also acquainted; he didn't hesitate and quickly agreed to assist. He was to come to my home, once I explained what I needed to accomplish. I thought we had a plan. But for some unknown reason, this individual, who I found to be quite professional never bothered to show up, call, talk to me about any apprehensions he may have had.

I couldn't understand the problem for the life of me, still today, I'm baffled. I've never understood why he did not simply say, "That's something I cannot do." for whatever the reason. What has happened to good old honesty! Are we afraid of honesty?

Tell the truth until it hurts. Tell the truth and the truth will set you free. (2 Timothy
2:15); (John 14:6); (James 5:19).

God gave me the strength to persevere. For months on end, and from the early hours in the morning, I would arise, go down on my knees to get all prayed up, thanking the Lord for his favor and asking him for his blessings and wisdom. I worked until late nightly hours through the AM. I tinkered around with the computer each day researching, jotting down notes and going through trial and error.

The Lord laid it on my heart to just keep on going. And low and behold God created the miracle below:

My Blog:

Today when I speak in public, and I'm asked by people about my writing process; sometimes my audience finds it hard to believe me when I confess: "I didn't do it, I didn't write it. God did it all for me." And I truly mean it. I mean it because until this day, I wouldn't be able to explain how this miracle happen if my life depended upon it. All I know is that I give all the credit to our Heavenly Father and His favor in my life.

Connie Williams This Life: Through Grace Hope and Mercy

Faith is the substance of things hoped for and the evidence of things not seen. (Hebrew 11: 1).

Chapter 15

∞

A prince of a man came into my life through God's favor.

At the end of the summer in 1996, after returning home from my eight–week Fellowship at Headlands in Sausalito, CA, and leaving those tall palm trees where the weather was always beautiful, I was on fire to purchase a new home with a garage. I was thoroughly finished with scraping snow and ice from my windshield in the winter months. Consequently, while still teaching at Piedmont, I took a telemarketing job to supplement my teaching income and to "bank bucks" for once I found the new home.

After the end of the first month at the telemarketing job with Fair Vision Time Share, I met someone new.

As most know, telemarketing is a numbers game making calls from a list of clients to get customers to take a tour of a time share with hopes of getting the client to invest in the plan. For one contact call, a husband gave me the name of his brother, who happened to be Rob. Initially I got Rob's answering system and left a message. I said, "Hello, this is Miss Love, (I would never leave my real name just in case I called some crazy lunatic), I'm calling to offer you the chance of a lifetime—a free steak dinner and a free vacation. Sorry I missed you, and I'll call back tomorrow at this same time, six thirty. Thank you."

Two days later, I finally got the opportunity to talk to Rob; fortunately, he does meet all the qualifications: income, credit and debt history; work ethics and home ownership and SINGLE; so, I schedule a tour for him at Fair Vision Time Share. Three days after the tour, I made the routine follow-up call to him to determine if he enjoyed the tour and liked the services and if he's interested in investment. Rob's voice sounded a little southern and compassionate, which sparked my interest, but he confessed to having no interest in investing.

In our later conversation, he admits, "I took the tour and then I hung around the agency for a while trying to be a nonentity, pretending to read some literature finally realizing the clock said five-thirty and that I needed to leave for work. I was hoping for an opportunity to meet you. I thought they were going to throw me out. Finally, the woman behind the reception desk asked if she could help me, I asked her about you." He chuckled at himself. "She told me that you were at another location, so I left."

As I listened to his story, I felt flattered, and I felt that his story was touching—real—coming from a real man! And although it was a business call, Rob had the resourcefulness to express a personal desire. I liked that right away! In listening to him, I suddenly realize, I was enjoying myself. I was enjoying his appealing tone.

I'm imagining him sitting there at the time share headquarters perusing magazines nonchalantly and trying to inconspicuously eyeball the women while wondering and trying to figure out which one I might be—I'm delighted!

After a while, I needed to end our conversation, so I asked Rob for a referral, which he quickly complied. What we shared in that unprompted exchange sparked an interest strong enough that we both wanted to and we agree to talk again.

In North Carolina: God sent a soul mate into my life. This photo is of our wedding day twenty years ago.

What I didn't know was that Rob had seen me in Sugar Creek Park in 1980 years before the time share tour. But he didn't share with me, and I wouldn't find out until sometime later that he fell in love with me the first time he saw me in the park, walking Miss Beasley, my Weimaraner, a female large hunting dog with a shorthaired silver-gray coat, belonging to a breed originating in Germany.

Over the next week, I managed to contact him, and we interviewed each other with the usual questions: Are you a religious person? Do you believe in God? Do you smoke? Do you use any type of drugs? Have you been married? Do you have children and if so, how many? Like me, Rob was a divorcee, but he was living on the south end of the city. During the conversation we made delightful discoveries about our commonalities, we both came from large families, we love the sport of tennis and we both love to competitively move the chess pieces around on the board.

I already knew he was a single man, and I knew his work history and his income because of the required application he completed to attend the Time Share.

After making my telephone number available and a lengthy period of telephone tag; teaching and telemarketing didn't leave much time for leisure and socialization during the week. House hunting and the usual chores of shopping, cooking cleaning and of course church attendance consumed a large portion of my weekends. So finally in the farthest lot of my life Rob and I managed to squeeze in some evening telephone dialogues and especially after his tennis buddy called to leave a message on my answering system confessing, "This is Jerome, a friend of Rob's, he wants to talk to you," I soon returned the call and we later agreed to go out on a blind date.

Finally, one evening after telemarketing, we met at one of the local restaurants, Grady's, in East Charlotte for our first date. Grady's had great food and service. That was back when Eastland Mall was the heartbeat and one of the places to be on the eastside.

As an English teacher, I must admit, (and I realize it's wrong to a certain degree), but if I meet someone, I'm always watching and listening to hear if the man is going to turn into a jerk—breaking verbs, blundering and falling over his own two feet, spilling the water at the table or unable to read a menu, the wine list, etc. But his man has done his homework; I thought at first. However, I soon discovered that this was his forte. I observed him order the wine with exquisite culinary knowledge and timing; he did not forget his class. He flashed a charming smile in my direction, "What would you prefer?" He inquired. I was instantly impressed by his sophistication, and by the manner in which I was respected.

On our second date, Rob went all out to impress me with his appearance. Again, we met at the same location, Grady's. I arrived early because I wanted to see what I was about to get, I wanted to see him walk in. I was not disappointed! I relished every minute of his entrance. He walked in with his chest stuck out, and I caught sight of what was obviously a fresh lowly trimmed haircut with a part in his hair that was striking. His gray sharkskin two-piece suit and round neck black shirt was fitting like a glove. When he saw me, I couldn't help but grin like a silly teenager as he moved in my direction. I recall saying to myself, "IS ALL THAT FOR ME? Well HELLO and Thank you Jesus!"

The rest is history; we soon fell head over heels in LIKE!

In the meanwhile, I did locate the new dream home in an appealing neighborhood. God is so very awesome—He allowed me to sell the Condo without having to place it on the real estate market and show it to strangers. Ironically, the builder of the new home bought my Condo and I purchased "The Carolina" the new house his company built, which included all the amenities I had prayed for and much more: Oversized two car garage—no more scraping windshields during the winter for me; master suite with whirlpool garden tub; wrap-around porch (I imagined my parents, especially my dad sitting out waving to the neighbors). Only God creates these kinds of miracles!

Seven months later Rob dropped to one knee brought out the diamond ring from his pocket he had chosen from Brownlee Jewelers and proposed.

Following our three weeks of pre-marriage counseling "Fulfilling our Biblical Roles as Husband and Wife in the Family" with Reverend Donnie Garris at Antioch Baptist Church, three years of dating passed swiftly before we were married. My grandson Dee escorted me down the aisle to the tune of K-Ci and Jo Jo's "Tell me it's Real" at Antioch, Rob's church, with our family and friends in attendance. At that time my dear father's rheumatoid arthritis was critical, consequently, he was unable to attend. My daughter the late Camille was my maid of honor. Rob's two brothers were attendants, and of course along with Jerome his best friend and tennis buddy. As I write this account of our lives, I can't help these overwhelming feelings of how God has blessed us with a twenty year marriage.

Ironically, it was some years later that Rob shared his story of how he felt the day he walked his dog Ginger, when he first saw me in Sugar Creek Park. And after initially seeing me, he continued to go there, hoping to see me again.

As Rob delighted in recounting the story, he actually described what I was wearing, He said "You had on green UNCC tennis shorts and shirt, little short footie socks with the ball at the heel and tennis shoes." (I took tennis lessons at Cal State back in the day, and continued to play over the years).

He told me he said to himself, "She talked to me and didn't seem 'stuck up and afraid'; she seems nice."

Consequently, he had no way of knowing that at the time I had just recently returned to North Carolina from my California Fellowship at Headlands, so I still had that "free spirit flair from the West Coast" instinctive ability to appreciate or make good use of something, and I was teaching school and taking classes at UNCC to get a Master's Degree. I wasn't naïve though, as I had been before because the "Mall stalker" incident had taught me a valuable lesson—so I was constantly watching as well as praying.

And now as God would have it, years later, from when we met on the blind date, the circle has been completed. He recognized in his heart and mind and confesses, "It WAS you that I met in the park those years before; I would recognize that "shake" anywhere."' His instincts to find me, and his timing were correct.

Connie Williams

This Life: Through
Grace Hope and Mercy

I thank God each day for this gift to me.
I pray for Him to allow me to treat Rob
well. He is a prince of a man—a partner,
who supports my God-given talents of
teaching and writing so it can manifest,
and he does not try to take that space from
my head—perfect NO—neither one of us is a
perfect being! But, a God-fearing partner and
prince of a man—YES!

Chapter 16

∞

It's me, it's me, it's me O Lord, standing in the need of prayer. It's me, it's me, it's me O Lord, standing in the need of prayer.

Not my mother, nor my father, but it's me O Lord, standing in the need of prayer.

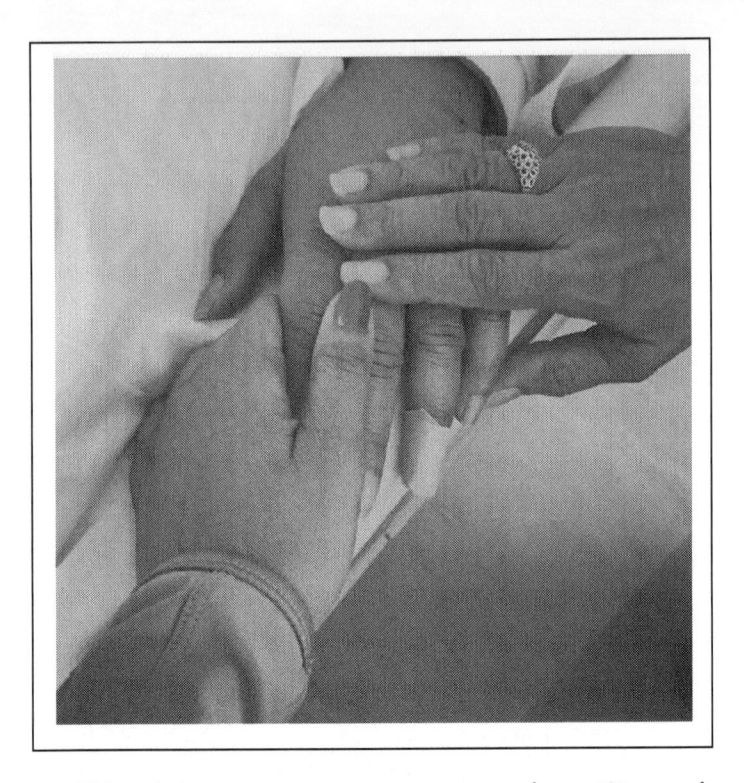

The three generations: granddaughter, Kate, her mother Raven, and me at CMC Hospital in ICU.

> Put the Lord in remembrance of
> his word. And call upon me in the
> day of trouble: I will deliver thee, and
> thou shall glorify me. (Psalm 50:15)

God's gifts: Raven and family

Raven has given us one granddaughter, two grandsons and one great-grandson.

God's gifts: Pricilla husband and family.

Pricilla has given us five grandchildren: three grand-sons, two granddaughters, five great-granddaughters and two great-grandsons.

God's gifts: Beloved Dawn and family

Dawn gave us two grandsons: three great-granddaughters, and three great-grandsons.

Connie Williams · This Life: Through Grace Hope and Mercy

God's gifts: Beloved Camille husband and family

Camille gave us three grandchildren: two granddaughters, one grandson and one great granddaughter.

****

There have been times in my life when I've felt that I can almost compare myself to Job from the Book of Job in the Bible. **Job** (a righteous man whose faith withstood every severe testing by God that describes Job's afflictions and eventual reward).

Of all the life-changing and testing by God experiences I've witnessed, there have been six that have shaken my world to its very core. I will continue honoring my Lord for his goodness and mercy in saving my life. Although the losses of my wonderful parents, Jones and Lillie Williams after their sixty-eight years of marriage, was painful, even though they both lived long lives and passed away at age eighty-seven and ninety, yet nothing can compare to the shocking losses of my two lovely daughters; my knee-baby, Dawn, at age twenty-two who went home with Jesus after a tragedy; the loss of my baby child Camille at age fifty, the loss of my dear grand-son Conner at age twenty-two; the unexpected loss of my sister Ailey at age sixty-four, who always had such high regards for me, and the almost loss of my oldest daughter Raven at age fifty-seven.

Lovely, swan-like Dawn had just been home for a visit in North Carolina only one year earlier at twenty-one when her life was taken, (and not until now, I've never been able to say this) one night in Dallas, TX. At age twenty-two, my poor little angel

Dawn happened to be in the wrong place at the wrong time doing the wrong thing. But thanks to our Almighty God, He holds her blameless. The lovely Swan-like Dawn was laid to rest near her grandparents on both her mother's and her father's side at Hillcrest Memorial Park in Monroe, NC. She is now in heaven with our Father.

When driving home on the long-isolated road late at night when I taught school at Piedmont High School in Union County, when coaching the cheerleaders after a basketball game; I have felt Dawn's angelic spirit in the back seat of my car looking over my shoulder protecting me to make sure I arrived home safely. On that particular time, I told her, "Dawn, I know that's you back there. I'm so glad you're here with me." And I would feel so incredibly safe.

And the second soul jolting experience was the loss of my baby child Camille at age fifty who was a diabetic with type-two diabetes and who went home to our Heavenly Father while visiting her sister in Los Angeles, CA one night while she lay sleeping. Camille attended schools in the Valley, California, and the Pontiac School in Michigan. As a wife and mother, she shared this love for her children with her husband Aldean. Camille had an incredible sense of humor. My brother Chet shared these words about her: "Camille always had a sweet and quite disposition. She was affectionate and put everyone around her at ease with her love and caring. She had a vast and warm heart that drew everyone she met closer to her. I will miss her strong and steadfast spirit, her beauty and her quiet calm that made everyone love her...I am comforted knowing that she is at rest, at peace and at home with our Lord. We will see her in heaven..."

My angel was laid to rest in Glen Haven and Shalom Memorial Park, Lopez Canyon, Sylmar, California where she grew up in the Valley.

Pricilla tearfully called one afternoon to inform Rob and me that her son Conner who lived with his grandparents in Quarts Hills, CA was gone. Young Conner was a college student in the Valley and had a somewhat quiet and shy demeanor. I truly believe he had been bullied at school, but he kept it inside and neglected to open up to talk to his family.

Of course, when we received the painful news, we took the next flight rolling and headed for Los Angeles to console Pricilla, her husband Clint and their other four children. Ironically, Rob and I had not long been to CA on a visit where we spent time in the Valley with Conner, his parents, grandparents and his siblings. We miss this beautiful, quiet and computer-savvy young man so desperately.

The last core shaken event was the close--almost loss of my oldest child Raven at age fifty-seven who is also a diabetic and whose blood sugar elevated to 1700, and her breathing and heart stopped.

The telephone call came in at approximately two-thirty in the afternoon. My husband Rob and I had just celebrated our birthdays, his was April 30th, and mine on May 5th. We celebrated by hearing and receiving the Word at the 10:45am worship service at Ebenezer Baptist Church and then we continued our celebration over a chicken, shrimp and linguini dinner at the Macaroni Grill. Our spirits were high and it was a bright and sunny day that the Lord had made. During the service, we both had turned our telephones off and neither one of us had turned them on again.

But shortly, as it happened, after dinner and before arriving home as we rode down 485, we both turned our telephones on again and there were several urgent messages. The first call said: "Mommy, Raven is in the hospital. Call me immediately!" The second one said, "Mommy, answer the phone, Raven is in the emergency unit University Hospital. Call me right away!"

The message on Rob's telephone said something of the same. "Call immediately! This is Pricilla."

We didn't go home. Rob immediately turned the car around at Rocky River and headed directly to University Hospital to the Emergency Unit as I telephoned to talk to my daughter Pricilla.

When we arrived at University Emergency Unit and asked for our daughter, we were told to wait for the doctor to come and talk to us. It was a thirty-minute wait, which seemed like thirty hours.

In the meanwhile, Pricilla was frantic with her information. What she told us just didn't sound good at all. I couldn't help but "ball." I immediately called on my Lord our God to help us in between sobs and my husband trying to hold me up.

Finally, when Doctor Gonzales came to talk to us, we asked to see Raven. Before seeing her, we were informed that our daughter was not responding to any of the performed treatments. He said that her blood sugar had risen to 1700 and her heart and breathing had stopped, but they had managed to get a faint heart beat after performing CPR and she had been put on a respirator, a machine used in hospitals to maintain breathing for patients unable to breathe unaided. Still with everything they were doing, she was not responding, and we were asked to begin notifying the family. The hospital was in the process of moving her to the CMC East IC Unit in Concord, NC. Rob and I held tight to each other and again called on our Lord before calling our family members.

When we were allowed to see her, I held my daughter's hand, and it was cold to the touch and she was unresponsively lying there in a hospital bed with the respirator tube in her mouth and I Vs in her arms. It was such a painful experience for both Rob and me. We both stood there with tearful eyes and holding on to our beliefs, knowing that God would help us.

The doctor informed us of how her good companion and friend, an Army veteran, was able to administer CPR to start her heart beat until the medics arrived. She was placed in ICU and put on a respirator. She was in a diabetic coma. The doctors said she was unresponsive to any of the treatments and placed on an around the clock monitoring by the medical staff. But although the medical professional had done all that was medically possible.

God is the final doctor, and we prayed to prick His heart.

My praying family gathered around us, her sister Sweet Pricilla who flew in from Los Angeles even though her husband's father had died a day before; and Raven's daughter Kate flew in from

Rhode Island. My loving brother, Mac and his long-legged wife Minister Konya, brothers Chris, Chet and sister Shirley, my wonderful praying sisters, Gina, Trudy; and the Davis family, my nieces, Shemika, Salama and a host of my praying church families, Ebenezer Baptist Church prayed and visited us at CMC East and prayed; Mount Olive AME Zion in Monroe and other church families and friends. My Face book was filled with prayers and well-wishing friends praying for her recovery every single day from the beginning—day one!

Raven was placed on a twenty-four-hour cooling procedure to get her sugar level lowered. To say the least, we were all so afraid. We prayed to God to save her. She was given a head CT (EEG) to check swelling and stroke possibility. Her brain activity was tested. She was experiencing some kidney failure. Lebifed was administered to bring blood to the body. (Non-steroidal Anti-Inflammatory Drugs).

Praise God Almighty according to her test, there was no brain injury and she had not had a brain aneurism. But there was a small spot of blood on the brain and therefore given a transfusion to keep her brain from bleeding. Then she was placed on 72 hours care and watch in ICU.

Over the next three days we cried, watched and prayed constantly for Raven. Calls from the family and friends were nonstop. I'm sure we pricked our heavenly Father's heart in heaven. At first Raven was not responding to any treatments, then God made a miracle, she began to move her left arm when her doctor applied pressure.

While we stood at her bedside, at the new hospital CMC in Concord, God touched her and on day three God woke my daughter Raven up from a diabetic coma. She had no brain trauma. Over the next three days, she could sit up in bed, and once the tubes—the respirator was removed she could speak and soon began the rehabilitation therapy. Praise to God! She continues to improve.

> All of us said, "Hallelujah and praises
> to the Lamb of God."

During this time, I often talked to my Lord. I continued to ask him, "God, how much more can this little heart take?"

What have I learned from asking this question, and what have I learned from these experiences? What I do know is that what we experience in our daily lives is nothing compared to what our Lord Jesus Christ experienced when they nailed him to the cross.

My learning consists of the following: My future is in my hands as long as I keep God's

Commandments. All things work together for the good of the Lord as I abide in God's love, from the violence caused by Walter the ex-husband to the stranger at dawn standing at my bed.

> **No weapon** that is formed **against thee shall prosper**; and every tongue that **shall** rise **against thee** in judgment thou shalt condemn. (Isaiah 54:17).

Work hard – stay on the course, knowing that my Lord would bring me through no matter what my unfortunate mistakes were. Through God's Grace, Hope and Mercy, I was able to kick the gate of hell down, like possibly going to prison for taking someone's life, to kicking doors open when I fought for and allied college professors to write letters in support of an opportunity to educate my mind with a four year, undergraduate degree; and later an advanced college degree. As far as losing something, get another one ideology, of course nothing and no one can replace neither my precious children Dawn, Camille nor my parents and other loved ones. But I managed to love hard on the two children God has allowed me to now have in my life, especially when He recently saved my oldest daughter's life from a coma.

So, encourage yourself in the Lord at all times. Say what the Lord says. When we keep talking about what things are, they will stay the same. Believe what God promised.

> He promised: And **call upon me** in the day of trouble; I **will** deliver **you**, and **you** shall glorify Me. **(Psalm 50:50).**

I'm not totally burned out by life's many crises. My desire to preach—get a PhD at this time. The warning light in my life required me to take a good long look at what I have endured: Raising the children, getting an education, teaching high school; college professor; cheerleader coach, wife, mother, grandmother and great-grandmother. I look to examples of my siblings, coworkers, friends, —unlike me who's led a troublesome (however not chosen) life. I realize it's up to me to change it; screen calls; especially the ones that come in the middle of the night; or very early in the morning. I have come to realize; I must allow grown people to become responsible for their own lives.

I no longer sign for apartments and end up paying the rent when grown adults sit around not working because they "refuse to flip burgers for five dollars an hour; yet they will spend my hard-earned five dollars." I no longer answer the call to go out and bail grown people out of jail, I say to them "call your parents." All of this is self-preservation – changing destructive patterns. I've stopped being so available even to those who vow to love me.

A strong desire to go into the Doctoral Program, the ministry causes restlessness in my soul. I may or may not get there—I'll see how God leads me—see how he lays it on my heart.

In the meanwhile, I'll Praise—Thank you God. Laugh--it makes a merry heart; research says it releases healing agents. A part of this awareness of laughter came about a while back as I sat at the usual location when I'm not doing household chores or on my part-time job at the University. I was sitting at my computer when the telephone rang and the answering system kicked in grabbing my attention when the caller leaving a message said "This is President Obama." Like an idiot, I jumped up—snatched up the receiver to answer the call saying, "Hello!" "Hello!" as if the President was actually on the line and going to answer my hello. I'm so thankful God gave us laughter!

Pray and build up yourself in the most holy faith and feed your spirit. Be strong and courageous. Go to sleep and wake up on the words of God. Continue practicing seeing victory instead of seeing defeat. Have Faith; the things of the world will choke the word. Stay optimistic; don't dwell on things of the sins and mistakes of the past.

> God says, "**BEHOLD**! I am doing a new **thing**." He is calling us to come up and out of the ordinary.

God can out do the past. We all have things we wish didn't happen. Negativity will only bring us down. For example, When Walter was released from Soledad Prison, he came looking and found us in the San Fernando Valley. I was at work at the Record

Ledger in Tujunga. Raven opened the door, and he stood there, "Tell your mama I'll be back; and when I do, I'm going to kill all of you."

He didn't kill anyone that day because God didn't allow it.

Once I arrived home and telephoned him, I said, "If you're going to kill me then you had better get to killing. I would rather be dead than to live with you!" Besides, I later learned that my father had promised him, "If you bothered her again, I will go to the end of the earth to find you." Walter never threatened or bothered neither the children nor me again. Each time afterwards, when I would occasionally find myself in his environment, like at our daughter Pricilla's wedding, he couldn't apologize enough. And later, he wrote many letters of apology to me as well as to my parents, confessing how he wished he could have been as good to us as we had treated him. And although it's difficult to forget such tragedy, thanks to God, He has allowed me to forgive him. And I make a conscious effort to never talk against Walter to our children. They want to love him; he's the only father they have.

So, go and be a blessing to someone when experiencing feelings of despair; and keep moving toward a goal, something you want to accomplish. Exercise and examine your eating habits—your daily consumption of food and the dynamics of your feelings. Get a friend and be accountable.

> A friend loves at all times, and a brother is born for a time of adversity. Proverbs 17:17)

Chapter 17

∞

What more can I say about God's favors and what I have come to know: In the Inductive Method of Study at Ebenezer Baptist Church, according to Kay Arthur, *How to Study Your Bible,* it is a study designed to draw Christian teachers into personal interaction with the Scripture and thus, with the God of the Scriptures so that the beliefs are based on a prayerful understanding and legitimate interpretation of Scripture-truth that transforms one when lived by it.

An Inductive Study on John 15:9-11 As the Father has loved me, so have I loved you. Now remain in my love. If you keep my commands, you will remain in my love. God is the true vine and His Father is the gardener. If we stay connected (keep God's Commandments) to the vine=God, then we will bear fruit. In other words, have a successful and productive life. The Vine and the Branches: "I am the true vine, and my Father is the gardener. He cuts off every branch in me that bears no fruit. (John 15:1-11)

> Depend on God for everything to bear fruit. If you remain in me and my words remain in you, ask whatever you wish, and it will be done for you. (John 15:7)

Shortly after the 1989 publication of my fictionalized autobiography, *Emily's Blues*, the Ebenezer Baptist Church in Charlotte sponsored a book signing on Saturday afternoon in 1991, and in 1993 the Ebenezer Baptist Church Missionary Circle president, Mrs. Bernice Douglas invited me to "deliver the message" to the church congregation on behalf of the 45th Annual Mission's Day celebration.

Connie Williams This Life: Through Grace Hope and Mercy

Mrs. Bernice Douglas   March 20, 1993
----- Fannie Circle
Charlotte, NC 28205

Dear Connie,
   Thanks again for so graciously accepting our invitation to be the guest speaker for Annual Missions Day. We look forward with great anticipation, because we are confident that with your experience as a writer and author, you will have a message for our congregation. Please send a brief biography sketch and the amount of your fee.

                                    Yours in Christ,
Mesdames Bernice Douglas, Naomi Love, Lillie Fair, Program Committee

*****

Ebenezer Baptist Church Annual Missions Day..... Sunday, April 25, 1993
.....11:00 A.M.

Dr. A.B. Sutton, Pastor

Mrs. Lillie Fair, Presiding

Order of Service
Devotional Meditation Moments
Musical Selection
The Call to Sacred Worship
The Giving of Tithes and Offerings
Worship Through Proclamation

Introduction of Speaker..........Mrs. Margaret Ross
Musical Selection..........The Choir

The Message.........Mrs. Connie Williams

Response of Faith

Program Committee...........Bernice Douglas, Naomi Love, Lillie Fair

The following text is an adaptation of the sermon, I artfully articulated as I commemorated the mission, and the struggles of life experiences while growing up knowing the Lord. At the Grier Chapel pulpit on Beattiesford Road, the meeting place for Ebenezer Baptist Church, after a fire destroyed the church at the Elizabeth Avenue location, the focus of my story to a congregation of over three-hundred on Sunday, 1993, was the challenges of missions for the young and the old.

Introduction of the speaker: Mrs. Margaret Ross

Title: "My Story and Mission in Life"

To: Reverend and Mrs. Sutton, Good morning Ebenezer, this is a wonderful day. I am honored because I've been asked by the Missionary Committee to speak on behalf of Mission's Day. Well Ebenezer, I'm having a good time, and I hope you are enjoying this day that the Lord has made and will continue to praise it in the Lord's name as I speak today. Everyone has made this a joyous occasion for me, especially Mrs. Douglas and all of the Missionary Group number four members.

Again, this is a great honor.

Please pray with me Church: Dear Father in heaven please hear and accept my prayer. Allow it to fall upon your ears so that I can receive and continue to receive your graces. I believe in God the Father who gave his only son Jesus Christ, who suffered under **Pontius Pilate** (was the judge at Jesus' trial, and authorized his crucifixion during the 1st century) was crucified, died and was buried. On the Third day he arose, ascended into heaven, and seated at the right hand of God who shall come to judge the living and the dead. I believe in the Holy Ghost, Holy Mary mother of God; Father wash us clean with the Blood of the Lamb. Thank you, Father for life, family, friends and our jobs. Father, bless us all and protect us. Help me Lord today. Allow me to speak religiously, rationally, eloquently, coherently and confidently. This I ask in your precious name. Please accept this prayer. Amen.

I want you to know that I've come a long way in my life to get to this point, through half deserted street, dangerous landscapes holding unfriendly elements—North Carolina, New York, New Jersey, Washington, DC, and back to North Carolina and then to California and now home here among God's people in the Lord's house—Home! Some of you that have read my book and my poem know that this has not been an easy life—it usually isn't for most of us. And some asked, HOW DID YOU DO IT? I stand here to testify that the credit goes to God. I stand here on God's shoulders, for only He could have delivered me. And the thing about my story is—some said, I just couldn't have told all of that about myself. And my answer to them—IT'S MY LIFE! And if my life story can serve to benefit one person then it is worth the telling. You know, life stories can be amazing because when I said that, it seemed that everyone had a story that they were waiting to share. It opened up such lines of communications because my story addressed the universal themes of the human experience.

So, I want to tell the story of how I became reborn and reborn with a mission—and not the one that I thought it was.

Webster, a Christian, defines mission as the act of sending an assignment or task to be carried out. And according to the Bible: the mission of Christ is: Do God's Will. From the book of John (21: 15-19) I am Reminded that Peter was considered the Greatest missionary of all. God missions Peter to demonstrate his love by feeding His lambs and His sheep.

You see, I was a follower of Christ, and then I became unwise (I was lost for a while) And let me say that although I was lost—in other words, I lost God, but He didn't lose me. I was in God, but for a time I wasn't in God. I left God, but God never left me because that's the way God is. I know now that God had a mission for me—a mission that even I didn't know about. And this was hard for me to understand, because I wasn't swift or strong, and in case you hadn't noticed, neither am I very tall in height. I thank the Lord every day for the person who invented high heel shoes. And it's all right for me to say this, but don't you try it. You would be stepping on my toe! Anyway, God enabled me to endure to the end.

So, I'm trusting for your prayers and patience and indulgence as I proceed to talk from the premise of four ideas:

I. The follower – because I was brought up knowing God.

II. I became an unwise – (One might even go as far as to say that I was a Fool). I left Him but he never left me because of the MISSION He had for me.

III. The third idea is that I am found (It feels so good to be found). I am reborn, I am happy, I am blessed and undertaking the Christian Mission that God has for me.

IV. The Challenge that I bring before myself and the CHURCH family.

As a child I had a very close relationship with God. I think this is so important for young people. They should establish a close relationship with God at an early age. It's like planting an acorn seed that presses forward to become an oak tree. I grew up in a large family with five sisters and five brothers—the second to the oldest child. Can you imagine getting ten different opinions when you ask for advice. My oldest sister Pat and my sister Gail (God rest her soul) would have a humorous response—like, "Girl are you crazy, --have you lost your mind?" My oldest brother Donald, we call him the godfather, he would say, "Don't worry about it; I'll take care of it. No problem." Trudy's approach would be from the 'Book of Ruth.' Chet the business wiz would approach the situation from an executive point of view— "What are the pros and cons?" Jen the medical student would set a medical tone. "What are the doctors saying?" Mac and Chris would approach the situation from a biblical premise: "Let's see what the 'Word' says." Mark and Gina the Gemini's in the family; Mark would say "its yes and no"—and Gina would reply— "But it's no and yes."

My parents, who were married for sixty-eight years, the late Jones McConnie Williams, a lover of God, and the late Lillie Williams, my beautiful mother worked hard to give their children the necessities. We were brought up respecting our elders. My grandfather, Reverend Daniel Author Williams, was a Methodist minister. WE didn't have luxuries in those days, in the fifties. But my parents and grandparents gave us something money cannot buy. The first Bible verse I remember learning and having to recite at the table before a meal is "Honor thy mother and thy father and the days shall be long upon the land which the Lord thy God giveth thee." God says Honor thy mother and thy father... some young people couldn't care less about these words.

I can recall as a very young child getting down on my knees and asking God for something and having that thing or event manifest not long after asking God for it. So, I knew God at an early age. Young people I'm assigning this mission to you: know God; establish a close relationship with our Savior. It will be your saving grace in the long run of life. Psalm 50:15: And call upon me in the day of trouble: I will deliver thee, and thou shalt glorify me.

I was blessed because through my parents' teachings and examples, a positive attitude developed – an accepting attitude that would require me to respect my elders and that would allow people to help me. You know some young people of today think that they know as much as the older people that has been around for a long time. Some of them will go as far as to say, you can't tell me what to do. Some of us think that we can't accept advice from someone that didn't come from the right side of the tracks. And therefore, we cut off the help – the blessings that God intended. I think Arrested Development pays tribute to Mr. Wendal a bum with wisdom- most of us are just a paycheck away from homelessness. So, even a bum can have some good advice.

You know God's love and blessings transcends the bounds of understanding, and I believe that there are angels right here on earth, and I believe that God places these angels along the way throughout our lives to help look after his sheep. But if we go around telling folk that they can't tell us what to do, then those angels won't be able to help us. I think back over my life and I see many angels, my parents who brought me up right, taught me to have a positive attitude. The picture of my mother's face comes to mind. She was always smiling, persevering, and not allowing negative events get her down. I truly believe this developed through the kind, loving attitude of my parents, especially my mother. She didn't have time to be sad, because she had eleven children to care for and a husband that was coming home looking in the pots and pans for a home-cooked meal. He didn't stop at McDonalds, Hardees, and Burger King. He came home for his meals.

I hear so many times about fathers leaving their children to be raised by the mother. And I believe this is so unfortunate – because I believe, and research shows that a child's conscious is developed through the loving relationship of the father. I remember being spanked only once by my father – now don't get me wrong. Mama loved us too, and was always there. But Mama would tear you up. But that one spanking by Daddy was such a shock that I carved the date on a tree in the backyard and vowed not to come inside until Mama returned home from work. My father was the kind of person who talked and reasoned with his children. That enabled us to earn his love and respect.

I see the angel Mrs. Lula B. Sims, third grade teacher and my mother –in-law. I married her son when I was only fifteen years old. She came to me one day and said, "If you go back to school, later in life you can be a school teacher too." Now if I had not had a positive attitude and not been accepting of her words, they would not have meant a thing to me. Instead, I weighted those words as being important. Plus, I had an opportunity to observe how she lived. She was a Christian and I admired what she represented. I'm glad that I didn't say, now who does she think she is telling me what to do. I'm grown. I KNOW what I can do!

I think of the angels, Mr. and Mrs. Neusom, a retired teacher and her husband, a retired Los Angeles attorney. There I was in California away from my parents and family, and looking for a place for my four children and me to live. You see, the marriage of ten years had dissolved. These people took a look at me and said, "You don't need to be in an apartment all by yourself. You can stay right here with my husband and me. And I did, with my children. Now there again, I could have thought that they were trying to KEEP ME FROM HAVING MY FUN.

I think of another angel, Dr. George Herrick, my old English instructor at Los Angeles Valley College in Van Nuys, a Euro American. He made sure that I knew about every opportunity a little poor African-American girl could need.

You see CHURCH, young people, God provided these angels along the way. But the important idea is that I had to have the attitude necessary to allow these angles to help me. This is the only way it could come about. He put them there. Make this your mission people; acquire a positive attitude that will enable people to help you. And sometimes that help comes in the way of some simple advice that is not to be underestimated either. I'm reminded of my grown children, and especially my baby daughter, God Rest Her Soul, who lived in Michigan, who asked me before she passed, when she learned of my speaking engagement, she said to me "Be sure to talk of how you mission us, your children each time we talk, by asking us to be the best Christian we can be.

With all to these angels, this positive attitude—God allowed me to acquire knowledge. I was like Eve in the Garden of Eden. God told Eve not to eat of the forbidden fruit. Well, you know, God is a jealous God. And when He says not to have any other Gods before me, he means that. I was so blessed, so knowledgeable, so well liked, that I became so wise that I was unwise. I became in other words, a foolish person.

Now when I say I lost God and became foolish, I don't mean that I became a thief, or a murderer, a drunkard, or a dope user of pusher, an abuser in any form. No! I didn't become any of those. And some of us seem to think that because we don't do any of those things, that we're okay. You see my sin became knowledge. I became big and important. I began to question, why is there suffering? Why is there pain? I questioned the validity of His words. I began to think like some of our young people today. In the words of Ms. Jackson, "What have you done for me lately?" I was like some of us, I knew too much for my own good. It is as if my eyes were closed. In other words, I didn't know what I didn't know. **That frontal lobe of the brain wasn't yet developed**.

I lost God in my life. I was foolish but I didn't know it. Now you know that is a sad thing—looking back retrospectively, I can't help but chuckle at my ignorance and how I must have looked and sounded to people around me who knew God. But I also lift my head and say thank you Jesus for saving me! Thank you, Jesus, —Thank you Father—Thank you Lord—Thank you God! I'm talking about myself, but I could be speaking of some of YOU!

I'm so glad God didn't lose me, I lost him but he didn't lose me because that's the way God is. I'm found, happy and doubly blessed. You see, I could be found because I was brought up knowing and loving God—the seed was always there because it was planted at a young age. I'm a mother, grandmother, and great-grandmother and trying with all my effort to live the mission. The mission is simple and clear, and as I stated earlier not the mission, I thought it was. You see while I was lost, I thought my mission in life was to GET A GOOD EDUCATION, SO THAT I COULD EARN A GOOD LIVING, BUY A BIG HOUSE, DRIVE A FANCY AUTOMOBILE, (You know when you pay the upper dollar amount, it is no longer just a car—it becomes AN AUTOMOBILE) WEAR EXPENSIVE CLOTHES (I LIKE VERA WANG) LOOK GOOD! Well, getting an education is important, and earning a good living is equally important, God wants us to live well. But more important is God's mission, and that is to be the best Christian that I can be and do God's work so that my life and my ways can glorify God and be an example for others, especially the young people.

    We as adults can no longer pay lip service, the old saying "do as I say and not as I do." Young people are listening to our words. And more than that, they are watching us, our actions and how we live our lives. Our young need role models that are within reach in the present environment that they can see, and touch, and talk to, not the super stars that they see on television and in the movies. Don't misunderstand me. I don't have anything against our young millionaires Cam Newton or anything against "Bouncy", Oprah and Tyler. The point here is that our young people are watching US. They are reaching out to US and seeking behaviors they can emulate. If they want to be teachers, they need to be around those in that profession; if they want to be doctors, they should emulate those in that profession, a lawyer, a preacher and so on.

    I challenge the CHURCH members to find a way to win the favor of our young people. If one of them do something we do not like, something we know is wrong, or we see them conducting themselves improperly or acting ill mannered, let us not stop talking to them. Let us give them a chance. They are young; so, let's find a way to lead them into our churches, into proper conduct, to close the gap between our differences and our likeness. Let us make it our mission to help them feel that no one is born on the wrong side of the tracks because we are all children of our Father. I realize that in this mission, I still have a long way to go. There are some areas that can stand improvement, but I believe God is working with me, and I know I am willing to let Him use me for his purpose. I challenge Ebenezer to find a way to win the favor of young people. We owe it to our ancestors, Frederick Douglass, Malcolm and Martin and others, who have worked and died for our lives to continue in this country to make it our mission to find ways to save our young people, to find ways to help them come to church, feel a part of the church family, to close the gap between the age differences of our deacons and those young aspiring deacons, between our ministers and those young aspiring ministers and right on down the line of succession. Make it our mission to let our lives and the way we live become examples so that we as older people know that our country, our homes our neighborhoods and our churches are in good hands. Let me see your hands CHURCH if you are willing to do this. Can I get an Amen?

And while the older people are carrying out these missions, I challenge the young people to make it their mission to adopt a positive attitude, allow these angels to help, talk, advice, and direct you. To choose Christ and his mission over disobedience, disrespect, drugs—choose love over hate. Choose as the movie producer Spike Lee says: do the right thing—doing the right thing in life. Are you willing to do this? Young people can I see your hands. Amen.

I know if we all work together to carry out God's plans, I believe this God given earth can and will be different.

Let us make it our responsibility to let our lives and the way we live become examples to our young so that we as older more experienced people know that our country, our homes, our neighborhoods are in good hands.

April 26, 1993

Dear Connie,
    Thanks again for that most challenging and inspiring message. We will always remember it.
        Sincerely,
        Bernice Douglass

****

Testimonial Speech: Delivered at the Horton –
    Blackmon Family Reunion, Charlotte, 2005.

Introduction of the speaker: Mrs. Betty Horton

Title: "My Story and Inheritance of Family"

Good afternoon. I'm honored to speak on behalf of the Horton Blackmon Family Reunion

    Please pray with me: Our Father in heaven please hear and accept my prayer. Thank you, Father, for this life; and allowing us to come together as a family. Father, bless us all and protect us as we bring the Horton-Blackmon Family Reunion to a close. Help me Lord today to speak rationally, eloquently, coherently, confidently and religiously. Thank you, Lord, for your blessings in Jesus name Amen

Today we want to reflect upon the inherited blood that runs through the veins of this family that we are born into and are still a part of, most certainly the handed down ideas, influences, the soul and the progress is still whole and remains stable.[1] We give tribute to our more mature members, our mothers, fathers, grandparents, our aunts our uncles and our cousins, have come this far by faith.[2] We want to give a promise to our young, yes, the generation of our children. That where there is a family in Christ there is strength. [3]

We cannot forget how fortunate we are, unlike the children in Africa and third-world countries, less economically advanced countries Asia, and Latin America who are in desperate need of school uniforms, books, supplies and teachers. So, in the mist of this cultural celebration, we realize that we have come this far by Faith, **but** we must remain humble and responsible to the inherited blood and the soul, the handed down ideas, influences and the progress. When I say responsible, I am referring to Our loyalty to our God given **Mission** in life.

I'm reminded of Paul in his mission to Titus who was under him. Chapter 2:11-13 - For the grace of God that bringeth salvation hath appeared to all men. Teaching us that, denying ungodliness and worldly lusts, we should live soberly, righteously, and

Godly, in this present world; looking for that blessed hope, and the glorious appearing of the great God and our Savior Jesus Christ.

In 1989 I felt compelled to write about my hardships and struggles. Some have read my book *Emily's Blues* and my poems know that this has not been an easy life—it usually isn't for most of us. Some have asked, how did you do it—escape from the dangers of crime, drugs, violence—SO FAR AWAY AND ALL BY YOURSELF? I can testify that the credit goes to God and the inherited effects of the family—coming up as the off spring of Jones and Lillie Williams in a household of eleven children, the expectations were founded on the WORD (the Bible's words) were communicated to us on how we were to conduct ourselves or we were surely to feel the wrath first of GOD and secondly we would feel the wrath (the belt) of Lillie Mae as well as have to endure the vernacular of Jones McConnie. Not like in today's society where spoiling the child and sparing the rod is the common thought practices, no, NO, in our house it was just the opposite. On a modern day note, if you ask me, that's what's wrong with people today! — unfortunately many of us haven't been educated, indoctrinated, initiated, nor edified—the benefits, especially of morally or spiritually, nor have they had the cultivation of the mind of the importance of the WRATH. For when I was coming up—in our house Mother's and Father's words after the Lords words reigned supreme—when they talked you listened—and you did what you were told! Or you knew the WRATH was sure to come! The consequences of your behavior!

> Honor thy mother and thy father.
> (Ephesians: 6:2)

In the telling of my story: *Emily's Blues* and my life—some said and some say, I just couldn't have told all about myself. And my answer to them is—it is my life. If my life story can serve to benefit one person, then it is worth the telling. Stories can be amazing because when one person opens up it causes others to open up to such communication, sharing their own stories. So, I tell the story for the benefit of our young people so they can know how I carried the inherited ideas and values of the family by adhering to God's mission in my life.

As I reflect back on my grandfather, Reverend D.A. Williams, the old home still stands on a triangle of land at highway 74, 200 and 218. But today there is a for sale sign on the property. Yet the sign does not diminish the love, the teachings, and the life blood continuing to run through a generation of over two hundred great-grandchildren, three hundred grandchildren and the fifteen children him and

Grandma Addie raised, one of which was my father, WWII Army Veteran Jones McConnie Williams.

In the forties the fifties and sixties, times were hard and money was scarce. Of course, money is scarce now, but not in the manner it was then. But my parents, they gave us something money could not buy. They taught us first to love God and obey his words.

As a young child, I knew what it meant to pray, to go down on my knees to God for something and having that thing or event manifest not long after asking God for it. So, I knew God at an early age. Young people I'm assigning this mission to you: know God; establish a close relationship with our Savior now in your life. It will be your saving grace in the long run of things.

The picture of my mother's face comes to mind. She was always smiling, persevering, and not allowing negative events get her down. I can recall her sitting in the dark room telling us our favorite childhood story. The room was dark because the lights had been turned off before my father could get off from work and get downtown in time to pay the bill. But Mama kept the faith so her children would not be afraid of the dark. So, through my mother I developed a positive attitude—an accepting attitude that would allow people to talk to me and advise me as I was growing up.

Many or our young seem to express impatience when their elders try to advise them. Technology has influenced this paradigm. They have grown up with the I-Pad, the I-Phone, and all the technology that many parents don't necessarily understand. They think their parents are not modern—not hip—not in vogue!" Some of our youths have the attitude, "You can't tell me anything- or what to do, and I'm grown." They questioned the validity of God words. God says Honor thy father and thy mother. Then as soon as something happens—the first thing they holler, "Help me Mama—Help me Daddy!"

Some people think that they cannot accept advice from someone that did not come from the so called the "right side of the tracks." Yet they believe what Sniff Pup, Hefty Jim, and Twenty-Five Quarters are telling them, and what they are telling our young will most likely only get them into trouble. Especially if they open that "thing" up, and let it fall because it's steaming. Well people, as a follower of God, don't cut off your blessings that are being provided. By having a positive attitude when your elders, our mothers and fathers, grandparents talk of their ideas and influences of the soul and their very own experiences that help us know where we came from and their mission in life, take it upon yourself to listen with an attentive ear. These are angels that God gives us right here on earth.

I was so blessed; there were so many angels as I was maturing, and of course I did possess an inherited positive attitude, and God allowed me the privilege to matriculate into the University at Cal State and the University at UNCC and acquire a formal education of sociology, psychology, botany, zoology, geography, literature and the like—book learning. I spoke the King's English as well if not better than the king himself. I knew how to conjugate the verb, the writing process, algebra, statistics and could teach anything I could read. I was almost like Eve in the garden. You know the story. God told her not to eat of the forbidden fruit on the day she did she became wise. With all my knowledge, as Jones McConnie would say, "with your know how, your ingenuity," I became so wise, that I was unwise. I became lost. Now when I say I was lost I mean I lost God and became foolish; I don't mean I would curse you out, tell a lie on someone, abuse and or promote the use of any illegal substances. And I felt that because I didn't do any of those things, I was alright. I began to question our Savior. I began to ask questions like, well if God is so good then why did this happen or why didn't that happen?

I began to question, why is there anguish? Why is there sorrow? I questioned the authority of God's words. I began to think like some of our young people today—the entitled generation; I want what I want now, give me my inheritance, what will you leave me in the Will? I was like some of us, I knew too much for my own good. It is as if my eyes were closed. In other words, I didn't know what I didn't know.

I was enormously foolish; I began thinking and feeling that man in some way is his own god. I stand here to tell you that we serve a mighty, mighty God who took care of this foolish young woman. (God will take care of you when you make the right decision and He will take care of you when you make the wrong decision.)

While I was lost, I thought my mission in life was to educate my mind to earn big bucks, look impressive in fine garments; buy a big house and drive a fancy car—live the good life. Well, God wants us to have nice possessions; He wants us to look prosperous too. I like Bandelino fashions! But more importantly is God's mission and that is to be the best Christian I can and do God's work so that my life and my ways can glorify Him and be an example to others by carrying myself in a way that exemplifies the inherited family ideas and values handed down to me.

God Will Take Care of You.
Hymn: Song Lyrics).

We see foolish young people and we certainly see some foolish old people too. Now that is when it is truly sad—to see an old fool who thinks he's smart. If you make an effort to inform them, to try and straighten them out, to try and tell them—you subject to get your feelings hurt. Now days unfortunately, you're subject to get "cussed out" in some language that can put the alley vagrants to shame--subject to get "beat down" and very possibly shot. Bottom line-- you will be told where you can go "wid dat." For example, advice to a grandson: He told me about his life up to this point in time: I'm thirty years old, I've been to the Air Force military, I've gotten my degree and I'm married and have a son, I'm a law abiding citizen and want to continue to have a relationship with you. You see I had reprimanded him for posting an (what I believed to be) inappropriate images and language on Face book. It was a situation to be handled with velvet gloves—a soft touch, because I didn't want him to withdraw—I did not want to jeopardize our relationship. I went directly to the scripture—I'm Grandma—it's my duty to advise my grandson (**Train up** a **child** in the way **he should go**, and when he is old, he will not depart from it) Honor thy parents--grandparents.

But, but, because I had established that close relationship with my God at that tender age, I had held on to those inherited influences that ran through my mind and trickled through my soul, I used the language of Jesus when he prayed: The language of Faith and Hope—not the language of doubt, fear and worry. So, I didn't worry about my grandson because I knew that he too knew God. So, Faith guided me and Hope sustained me.

We as adults can no longer pay lip service, the old saying "do as I say and not as I do." Young people are listening to our words. And more than listening to our words, they are watching us, our actions and how we live our lives. Our young need role models that are within reach in the present environment that they can see, and touch, and talk to, not the super stars that they see on television and in the movies. Don't misunderstand me. I don't have anything against our young millionaire ball players like Crowder from Monroe, or anything against those in the music industry, Ferrell Williams and P-Ditty. The point here is that our young people are watching US. They are reaching out to US.

I'll tell the story of a student in one of my English classes. We were studying values and norms. A value of course is something we believe in; a norm is rule—a law that can be backed by force and consequences.

This young man raised his hand, and I called on him. He said, "Do you know what I saw Ms. Williams do?" My heart sort of sank because I did not have a clue as to what he was referring. On the one hand I wasn't too worried because I knew that I was on the positive side of the law. However, there was something he was about to tell, and it did not sound that good at all. The young man continued, "I saw Ms. Williams turn into the parking lot the other day, and she did not use her turn signal. I sat right there in that cafeteria and watched her do that. **You have to follow the rules Ms. Williams.**"

I was glad that young man had expressed his observation in such an intelligent manner. I respected his words, and I did promise to use my turn signal whenever making a turn. I could have played it off, you know how we do our young people sometimes. I could have said, "Well, I knew what I was doing." But that young man probably would have lost respect for me because I did not reciprocate, receive what he said as important. Perhaps it would have been the one event that would have driven him away—he might have stopped coming to my class. Evidently, the inherited blood that ran in the young man's vein, and his positive family influences helped him distinguish between right and wrong. So, you see, our young people have their eyes on us, even when we do not realize it.

I challenge the family members to find a way to win the favor of our young people. If one of them do something we do not like, something we know is wrong, or we see them conducting themselves improperly or acting ill mannered, let us not stop talking to them. Let us give them a chance. They are young; so, let's find a way to lead them into our churches, into proper conduct, to close the gap between our differences and our likeness. Let us make it our mission to make them feel that no one is born on the wrong side of the tracks because we are all children of our Father and part of this family, this culture, this heritage. Let us make it our responsibility to let our lives and the way we live become examples to our young so that we as older more experienced people know that our country, our homes, our neighborhoods are in good hands.

And while the older people are carrying out these responsibilities/missions, I challenge the young people to make it their responsibility to adopt a positive attitude, allow your family and God fearing adults to advise and direct you to continue to carry out the handed down ideas and inherited influences of the family. To choose Christ and His mission over disobedience and drugs, choose as the movie producer Spike Lee says: do the right thing—doing the right thing in life. I believe that if we all work together this God given earth will be different for all the families, Not just the Horton, Black-man family, but the Williams, Massey, Sims, Stamps, Jordan, Wynne's, Erving, Winchesters, Colbert's, the Coffey and together we can bring others together. This way we all WILL make a remarkable difference.

****

Testimonial Speech: Little Rock AME Zion Church, October 5, 2017

Introduction of speaker: Reverend Glencie S. Rhedrick, M.S., M.DIV. First Baptist Church West, Charlotte.

Title: A Victim of Domestic Violence

I'm Connie Williams, author of *Emily's Blues*, *Green* and *Jon and Lale's Dance*, and the soon to be published, *This Life: Through Grace, Hope and Mercy*.

I feel it may be of interest that the public read about the life of a teacher, and today's time dictates that if this teacher is a female of color, an African

American, and victim of Domestic Violence perhaps the appeal will be even greater. I am a victim of domestic violence which lasted for nine years.

Today, I want to talk from my book, *Emily's Blues*, is a fictionalized autobiography about such a person written in ten chapters in 1989 and set in North Carolina where I was born.

As an African American writer, I believe I have a responsibility to help bring about an awareness of a certain criteria and caliber to our society.

One can survive the blues, domestic violence, abuse and neglect; I know this because I've survived it. I survived because of faith and favor through God.

I was married at age 15 and became influenced by my mother-in-law who was a Christian and a teacher, and she treated me like her own child. She said to me one day, "If you do this, and this, you too can become a teacher." You see I was the kind of girl that listened to those who wanted to advise me. As a teacher, my mother-in-law was off during the summer and she still had a check coming in the mailbox. I wanted to be like her. So, I didn't put my hand on my hip and say, "I'm grown, you can't tell me what to do."

By age 19, I had four children and had lived in North Carolina, New Jersey, New York, DC, and finally California where I managed to overcome. I became unstoppable in educating my mind and removing myself from an abusive situation—that wasn't easy.

Unfortunately, my husband became incarcerated and one day when I went to visit him at Soledad Prison, he sat behind bars; said to me, "You know I'm going to kill you when I get out." After suffering his violence, abuse and neglect against me for ten years, this was the deciding factor. I filed for a divorce the next week. I had no choice; it was the only way to remove him from my life.

In California, I repeat, I became unstoppable in educating my mind. I received a degree from California State University, Northridge in English and a Master's Degree in Education from UNC at Charlotte where I taught Composition, Inquiry and Rhetoric in the English Department.

Reading: Taken from the new work here: *This Life: Through Grace Hope and Mercy*: Chapter 1, PP 14 through 18 to the end of PP 2.

In closing: Violence only begets violence. In this experience, I wasn't trying to destroy my friend. NO! I was venting the internal rage experienced at a young age until maturity—a ten year period.

Following this discourse, the Captain of the Charlotte Police Department over the Domestic Violence Division took photos of my posters and invited me to speak to the Charlotte-Mecklenburg Students in Schools in the near future.

He confessed, "When I talk to students, they don't want to listen to me. But YOU, they will listen to you!"

Again, I'm being blessed. And I want to Thank my Jesus for being so good to me.

Chapter 18

∞

I must stay on the course, the path that leads me to glorify God. God will put you where He wants you to be even if others do not think you deserve it.

Oh, ye of little Faith: Ben Carson in his book *America The Beautiful* asked, "Does our religious "<u>belief</u>" divide us?" He goes on to admit, "As a Christian, I am not the least bit offended by the beliefs of Hindus, Buddhists, Muslims, Jehovan's Witnesses, Mormons, and so forth. In fact, I am delighted to know that they believe in something that is more likely to make them into a reasonable human being, as long as they don't allow the religion to be distorted by those seeking power and wealth." Those in positions of leadership in our society must familiarize themselves with the religions of all their citizens, and they must begin to emphasize the commonalities that unite us as people of faith.

Although Ben Carson asked: Does our religious <u>belief</u> divide us? I ask the question this way: "Does our religious '<u>faith</u>' divide us?"

What cause me to contemplate this question are three reasons: 1] the results of the Official Stewards apprehension about an intended Charity Performance of donated copies of my historical novel *Green*. [**Official Steward** works with the Pastor in the management of church-owned properties, investments, and the financial and legal matters].

Upon discussing the idea with a devoted Deacon, "IN THE PRESENCE OF MY DEAR HUSBAND AT THE CHURCH," we collaborated and determined the Benefit was a completely worthy cause and should possibly take place during the month of May, on Sunday mornings before and after the 10:45 a.m. worship service, and before the June CJ Golf Tournament because it too is an Academic Benefit. All proceeds from the Charity Performance would be given as an Academic donation and receipted as a contribution.

In our collaboration the devoted Deacon suggested; I was delighted and therefore did agree, that there should be a book signing by the author.

2] Further, what causes me to address this issue is that I am being led by the Holy Spirit, and it is a GOOD thing that our Lord has laid upon my heart.

I feel it necessary to identify a small part of my lineage at this point: I am from the Williams' legacy of Monroe, North Carolina. My father the late Jones McConnie Williams, WWII Veteran, attended Shaw University in Raleigh, NC, taught Upholstery Trade Arts at Winchester Center in Monroe, North Carolina, and at Central Piedmont Community College, and he and my beautiful mother, the late Lillie Williams were married for sixty-eight years and raised eleven children. My dad, like his brother, the late Andrew Williams were highly successful upholstery business owners in Monroe. Dad and his brother upholstered the whole town's furniture, including the school superintendent's. Ironically, the furniture in our house was often tattered.

My grandfather is the late Reverend Daniel Arthur Williams of Mount Olive AME Zion in Monroe,

NC; my grandfather's brother, Sikes Williams, who attended Johnson C. Smith University (Bittle College at the time) and North Carolina Central College was the first black teacher in Union County. Sikes Williams is the father of my cousin, the late Robert Franklin Williams, who was the president of the NAACP chapter in Monroe, NC, a civil rights activists and author of the renowned book, *Negroes With Guns*, New York: Marzani & Munsell: 1962 and Wayne State University Press: 1968. Robert F. **Williams**, "Black Power," - Purdue College of Liberal Arts .

Robert F. Williams' son is the late Reverend John C. Williams, pastor of Cass Park **Baptist Church in MI**. My cousin Haywood Redfern of Waxhaw, NC is a pastor in Monroe. My granddaughter's husband is Pastor M. Mitchell, of Kanisa Fellowship a contemporary Toronto Seventh Day Adventist Christian Church in Toronto, Ontario, Canada, and his father is the late Pastor Carlton Mitchell who served the Ontario Conference for 30 years. My cousin Reverend Thomas Mitchell is associate pastor of Torrance Chappell Baptist Church in Davidson, North Carolina.

Therefore, my love for God, theology, education and literature, the art of the written word, developed through the cultural ties of a strong family.

Those who know me as a life-long member of the Missionary Ministry and have read my works, *Emily's Blues*; *Green* and *Jon and Lale's Dance* can attest to my upbringing as one not based upon economically affluent means; however, a heritage based upon a love of God, the love of theology, the love of knowledge; I also have a love for the art of the written word.

With this love of God, theology, knowledge and the art of the written word, the literate individual's life derives its meaning and significance from intellectual, aesthetic, and spiritual participation in the accumulated creations and knowledge of humankind, made available through the written word (Scribner 1984). God had shown favor and allowed me to answer the missions in my life: to be the best Christian I can be to glorify Him; to educate those who thirst for knowledge; and to write books that enhance education: This authorship includes the three before mentioned books: *Green, Emily's Blues and Jon and Lale's Dance*. *Green* is especially designated for the Charity performance. Written with a double plot, it tells of the civil rights hero, my cousin and president of the NAACP, Robert F. Williams' (referred to as RW in the story), his struggle for equality and fight to save the lives of two little black boys that the town wanted to hang during the late 50s; and the book tells of the race upheaval of the early 60s set in the segregated South, Monroe, NC. RW escaped being hanged and he and his family had to go into exile—into Canada, Cuba and finally China—in other words, like the story of **Shadrach**, Meschach, and **Abednego** from the **Bible** book of Daniel 6, it tells us of three Jewish boys who refused to bow down to the King of Babylon; RW refused to bow down to the racists KKK in Monroe. God had to snatch **Shadrach**, Meschach, and **Abednego** from the fire and RW had to be snatched from the hanging rope. Also, in the story, our protagonist, a young girl of eleven, is searching for her identity while experiencing the harshness of racism and violence in her home town (Monroe). I wrote the book because it is based on a true story and because I believe there are not enough stories based on Black history and told by a young female.

In a blurb on the cover of *Green*, the son of Robert F. Williams, Reverend John Charmer Williams, my cousin, the late pastor of Cass Park Baptist Church, MI, says, "I believe the work will do great things for young audiences who otherwise would know nothing about Robert F. Williams, the civil rights activists. The history is relevant and important today."

I chose to give an Educational Endowment because of my academic background: A retired

English Composition and Rhetoric college professor from the University of North Carolina at Charlotte and a retired high school English instructor from Charlotte Mecklenburg and Union County Schools, with an advanced degree in Education from UNCC, and an undergraduate degree in English from Cal State University, Northridge.

I must credit my CHURCH for honoring me over the years, allowing my participation in numerous events with my works, such as: the Fall Festival; the Black History Program; Hattitude, the Homecoming event; Walking By Faith for which I am most grateful, and feel very Blessed by God. These programs were usually scheduled on Saturdays; consequently, the majority of the congregation is not likely in attendance.

As stated earlier in, TL: TGHAM, during the course of my writing experience I met the world-renowned Alex Haley, author of "Roots" and the *Autobiography of Malcolm X*. One piece of advice the late Mr. Alex Haley shared with me when I met him in 1990: He said "Be sure to preserve the history of your culture." In following Mr. Haley's advice, I wrote *Green* so that the story could be shared, and others could learn about the episodic occurrences of hate inflicted upon our people right down the road, in Monroe, NC, and the struggle my cousin, Robert F.

Williams endured while fighting for life, equality and Constitutional rights in North Carolina.

My book *Green* was so generously endorsed in Charlotte, North Carolina at Antioch Baptist Church by the Reverend Donnie Garris, the UMBA Moderator, who read the book, discussed that it is a "good read" and that it is set in his and my hometown of Monroe, North Carolina. He mentioned in his critique that he could identify with the locales and the storyline. At the end of his Sunday service he called me (Connie Williams, the author) up to stand beside him in front of the congregation so that members who desired to do so could peruse the book and purchase signed copies. I later gave a generous donation to Antioch.

A similar experience occurred at my grandfather, the late Reverend Daniel Arthur Williams' church in Monroe, North Carolina at Mount Olive African Methodist Episcopal Zion Church, now under the leadership of Reverend Brenda V. Harris. On the Sunday that my book *Green* was introduced to the members, the church was honoring their one hundred-five year anniversary and there were three guest ministers in attendance. Reverend Harris allowed me up to speak to the congregation whereby I introduced myself and my work. Then she proceeded to allow the congregation including the guest ministers (they all did purchase books as well) to purchase the copies which I personally signed for them. Following, I did give a generous donation.

Another experience of this type took place with my brother, Christopher Williams' church Blessed Assurance Faith Center in Charlotte, North Carolina, under Reverend LaVern Williams. At that particular time Reverend LaVern Williams was away. She had appointed my illustrious brother and graduate of Economics from East Carolina University, to preside over the service in her absence. Again, I and my book, *Green* were introduced to the congregation. Quality time was spent in a discussion and sharing of the story during the Sunday service.

Directly after publication, Henderson Grove Presbyterian Church, Charlotte, NC, adopted *Green* for "My Girl" a young church organized group of readers under the leadership of Reverend Sonya "Dino" Allen and her mother and father, my lifetime friends in Christ and education, Clarence and Ann McAuley.

And more recently, I have spoken at Little Rock AME Zion Church, at the request of Reverend Glencie Rhedrick of First Baptist West who read my book, *Emily's Blues* for which I am most grateful to God. My presentation was taken from the new work in progress: *This Life: Through Grace Hope and Mercy*.

3] My last reason for addressing this issue is that I believe, and I do know in my heart, God wants us to speak his language of Faith and Grace. He does not want his children to speak fear, doubt and worry. God allowed this gift of writing. I didn't choose it—it is a gift from our Father. (Philippians Chapter 1: V3-6) God started it, He inaugurated it. God will work with you, around, beside, behind and if not careful, without you! He started it to continuation—until it is completed. The outcome is going to be complete. There is no need to panic, nor worry. God will complete it.

Furthermore, *Green* is no stranger to our CHURCH. Many members including The Reverend and other ministers have purchased the historical novel. Many members have commented on the unbelievable and intriguing story. It would be an honor and delight for an opportunity to formally sign copies in an organized setting with the support of the ministers on the desired day and time—"Sundays before and after the 10:45 a.m. services." I had already asked permission from our good Reverend of the CHURCH, who granted with a smile, a verbal approval for this endeavor. Reverend did NOT say take the request to the Official Stewards of the CHURCH; he did not hesitate, nor equivocate, he said "Yes."

It was enlightening to learn that the Official Stewards could override a decision already granted by the PASTOR of the CHURCH. If in fact this is the case? Of course, I do comprehend as a retired teacher of Economics, Legal and Political Systems as well as English Inquiry and Rhetoric, that every institution, religious or otherwise have a checks and balance procedure much like the thirteen Cabinets of the US government.

Over the course of several weeks, I drafted the required emails to the appropriate CHURCH administrative authority to help expedite this endeavor, but It was determined that nothing of this type should take place on the First Communion Sunday; and nothing should take place on the Sunday for Mother's Day, consequently, the date needed to be changed.

This is when I was finally informed that the Charity performance needed to be approved by the Official Stewards of the CHURCH, and I was sent an "Official" Form which I completed and submitted in a timely manner for approval. Mind you, none of the other churches, Antioch, Mount Olive, or Reverend Williams' church, Blessed Assurance, where a detailed discussion about the subject ensued; they had not delayed my cause: Once the Pastor/Reverend granted their approval it was expedited in a short amount of time, whether the approval was written or verbal.

According to Hebrew 11:6, Prayer is the conversation, and Faith and Grace is the language of God. God does not speak the language of fear, doubt and worry.

Now again, I relate to the previous overwhelming question.

Did the Official Stewards unfortunately forget to speak God's language of Faith and Grace, or was the language negative—full of doubt, fear, and worry?

It was shared with me that there was a concern: My Endeavor Could /or Might "Start a Firestorm in the CHURCH!" If I am correctly informed, during the meeting there was an implication that other members of the CHURCH might become envious of what I was about to do. Mind you, [My endeavor was to: donate "free" copies, my historical novel *Green*, make them available to the congregation, volunteer my time to sign them and donate the proceeds to the Academic Sponsor] 1. How can anything about this cause a "firestorm" in the CHURCH I asked myself?

I am reminded of our study of *the Five Star Church* chapter 4, "Excellence as a Process"; Success is a journey not a destination. "(John 15): Jesus says He is the Vine and we are the branches, and if we abide in Him, we will bear much fruit. Our main goal as Christians should not be to bear fruit; it should be abiding in Christ, because if we do, we will bear fruit."

"We talked about this same idea in the context of ministry involvement. One of the most important reasons for Christians to utilize their spiritual gifts is that it helps them grow as they serve others..."

The Official Stewards' actions <u>seemed</u> to have been motivated by FEAR, DOUBT and WORRY: The devoted Deacon was, "one might say, <u>Warned</u>." [Warn=to notify or make aware in advance of something, especially of possible danger or misfortune] 2. The warning was: The devoted Deacon could move forward with the event if he wanted to, but to BE AWARE OF WHAT HE MIGHT CAUSE within the CHURCH. So again, the question occurs to me: "Are we divided by our <u>Faith</u>?"

Matthews: Chapter 6:5 Prayer: the Conversation of FAITH and GRACE.

Respond in Faith what Grace has already spoken.

First John: Chapter 17 John the gospel. Chapter 4: V 20. Matthew, Mark, Peter and John: Jesus praying; being led by the Holy Spirit.

If Jesus/God is led by the Holy Spirit, shouldn't we be led likewise?

It would have been an honor had the Official Stewards been led by the Holy Spirit and stepped out on Faith with Grace in support of the goodness the books could do for the entire congregation, especially the young.

Where I was invited to read, make the book available and sign copies, at The University of North Carolina at Charlotte's downtown campus, in their festival announcement of 5-6-17 by Dr. Mark Dunn, it was termed this way: "<u>The festival aims to bridge the university and city through the literary arts and celebrate all the many ways we tell stories, all at our</u> vibrant UNC Charlotte Uptown campus. <u>We hope attendees will discover how literature gives joy, unites communities, and expresses our shared humanity, as well as consider how writing and art can sustain a community, especially in times of change and upheaval.</u>"

As an abiding Christian of love, faith and hope; a person of sound ethos, pathos and logos— credible, caring and rational process of discussion and analysis.

It is my sincerest BELIEF and observation that the *Green* benefit would "NOT" have caused a firestorm of dissatisfaction at CHURCH in the least! I have HOPE in all of my heart it would have been endorsed well by the members of the CHURCH; it is my TRUST that the "MORALE OF THE CHURCH WAS COMPLETELY MISUNDERSTOOD AND UNDERESTIMATED."

Many of members already have the book, just as Antioch; Mount Olive AME; Blessed Assurance Faith; Henderson Grove Presbyterian Church; members of First Baptist West; West Boulevard Library; Hickory Grove Library; The University of North Carolina, at Charlotte; the Union County Library; the Charlotte-Mecklenburg Library; adoption by the McCrorey YMCA book club, Johnson C. Smith, James B. Duke Memorial Library, and members at Mount Carmel may introduce the historical novel. More recently, Johnson C. Smith Duke Memorial Library in 2018 has adopted three of my four published books: *Green, Emily's Blues and Jon and Lale's Dance. Confession of the Onion Ring King* had not yet been published; it was published in May of 2019.

I believe the reading of the historical novel; *Green* has the potential to assist understanding the perspectives of a part of our past. I have variously called this understanding, literacy as salvation and literacy as a state of grace—dignified, or grand way of doing something which helps connect us all through FAITH, HOPE AND TRUST, and; therefore, make us better. Although the signing of *Green* was not allowed at Ebenezer for this particular vendor, I still gave a generous donation in a signed check to the Scholarship Fund from AWAP my publishing imprint.

I can do all things [which He has called me to do] through Him who strengthens and empowers me [to fulfill His purpose—I am self-sufficient in Christ's (Philippians: 4:13).

For thou, Lord, wilt bless the righteous; with favor wilt thou compass him as with a shield (Psalm: 5:12).

Chapter 19

∞

Before my retirement/departure from the University of North Carolina at Charlotte, in 2014, I was invited for two consecutive years by Dr. Eddie G., a former administrator of Ebenezer and founder of the Theological Seminary School of Charlotte, to answer the call to teach English at his Seminary School; however, I respectfully declined because at the time I still had a professorship at UNCC; nonetheless, I left an open opportunity for a future consideration if the situation presented itself. Looking back retrospectively, I sometimes wish I had accepted the opportunity because it would have allowed a hands on approach to something that has been tugging at my heartstring—a calling to go further into the ministry. Now four years later since his offer and I'm experiencing a feeling of some kind of great loss. Sometimes when I think of what I neglected to act upon and sometimes I feel it's never too late. God has not laid it upon my heart as to what I should do. I'm waiting on the Lord to speak to my heart.

I was later asked to answer God's call to become a part of the EDI (Ebenezer Discipleship Institute/Bible Study) at my church: Ebenezer Baptist Church which was in need of more instructors, where I was once appointed First Vice president of the Missionaries by the late Roma Butler. I have taught Bible School, motivated youths to write and perform various plays including the Christmas play. I did respond favorably to this call. Refer to: Pedagogy I and Pedagogy II.

I wrote and submitted Pedagogy I and Pedagogy II to teach in EDI: *Imagine Your Life Without Fear,* Lucado, Max.[1] Pedagogy II Understanding Christian Ethics.

Understanding Christian Ethics, Tilliman, Jr. William, [2]

Pedagogy: I [1]

Title: Lucado, Max. *Imagine Your Life Without Fear*. Thomas Nelson, Nashville: 2009. ISBN 978-0-8499-2020-2.

Course 105: "Walking Boldly" Instructor: Connie Williams. Room 116. Time 7-8: p Wednesdays
Aim Use of the Text: *Imagine Your Life Without Fear*, **Lucado:** The anecdote to Fear is TRUST based on Scripture.

Objective: To invite and connect every person in America to a Bible-believing church, and ultimately into a personal relationship with Jesus Christ through Imagining Your Life Without Fear: "Walking Boldly." The anecdote to Fear is TRUST. If we trust God more, we can become fear less.

Connie Williams. Room 116 / EDI 105 Walking Boldly: Date_____

Our focus: Why Are We Afraid?

Course themes pg. 1-6: You are worth more than many sparrows.[1] God will always be with us.[2] We fear because this sounds too good to be true.[3] But when we fear we disappoint God[4] -when fear becomes worry[5]. We should not fear—we are God's masterpiece. [6]

Fear Knocks: P-7   (Matthews 14:27 NLT) Take courage. I am here. Dee's story: Fear and alcoholism.
Why Are We Afraid? P-13   (Matt. 8:26 NCV)
Does God Care?   P-20   (Matt.   8:25/   Matt. 4:23/8:16/) Fear not genre pg. 23/24.
The Ultimate Fear P-38   (John   14:1-3   NLT) Pg. 31=Philosophers myth about death.
Fear Not: God's Promise P-38   (Matt. 10:31 NCV) Pg. 38 We are God's masterpiece.

Closed question- remembered data	Open question-discussion and interaction – students generate own questions	Use the space to respond.

Extra space for writing answers above.

But Jesus spoke to them at once. "Don't be afraid," he said.
"Take courage. I am here!" On the passing John the Baptist.
behold, they brought to him a man sick of the palsy,
  The Death of John the Baptist. ... c **14:27**

28Then Peter called to him, "Lord, if it's really you, tell me to come to you, walking on the water."29"Yes, come," Jesus said. So, Peter went over the side of the boat and walked on the water toward Jesus.

Matthew 8:26-28New Century Version (NCV)
26 Jesus answered, "Why are you afraid? You don't have
enough faith." Then Jesus got up and gave a command to the
wind and the waves, and it became completely calm.
27 The men were amazed and said, "What kind of man is this?
Even the wind and the waves obey him!"

Application: Analysis
Synthesis
Evaluating
*We should focus on some main ideas from "Why Are We Afraid," Pg. 13-19.

- **John 14:1-3, New Living Translation (NLT)** "Don't let your ...
https://www.bible.com/bible/NLT/John.14.1-3
John 14:1-3, New Living Translation (NLT) "Don't let your hearts be troubled. Trust in God, and trust also in me. ... Read **John 14** Download The Bible App Now.

Matthews 10:31 NCV: Two sparrows cost only a penny, but not even one of them can die without your Father's knowing it. God **even knows how many hairs are** on your head. So, don't be afraid.

Matthew **10:28-31,** New Century Version **(NCV) Don't be ...**
https://www.bible.com/bible/105/*Matthew*.10.28-31.*ncv*   Matthew 10:28-31, **New Century Version (NCV)** Don't be afraid of people, who can kill the body but cannot kill the soul. The only one you should fear is the one who can.

Ephesians 2:10 New Living Translation (NLT) 10 For **we are God's masterpiece**. He has created us anew in Christ Jesus, so **we** can do the good things he planned for us. God said, "You are my poem…"

*We should focus on some main ideas from "Why Are We Afraid," Pg. 13-19.

We should focus upon the Thinking Skills such as: Analyzing=(underlying theme), Synthesizing=

(Can you see a possible solution), Evaluating=(Determine why people choose)?

Pedagogy: II [2]

Title: *Understanding Christian Ethics*. Fort
        Worth, TX: Broadman Press. 1988

Instructor: Connie Williams: EDI

Aim: Assist in understanding Christian Ethics.

Objective: Teach the thirteen chapter themes from Understanding Christian Ethics as they relate to the manifestation and accomplishments of an obedient and ethical Christian writer.

Reveal the testaments of the Holy Bible (Hebrew 13: V 5-6); Matt 1:18, 20 Luke 1 35)
Prov 8: 22; Wis 7-25-26 as they apply to walking in God's Words. Divine Ordering of our steps through Faith and Hope exemplified in intelligence=Wisdom: According to the *Invitation to the New Testament.*

Course themes (to lead to discussions)

1. Related to Christian ethical/ positive thinking [1] - (A Godly act, and the writing process - manifestation of the written work: novels *GREEN* and *EMILY'S BLUES*). Account of one's life and actions.

2. **God's Promise:** [2] I will never leave you (Hebrew 13: 5-6) Our Conduct is to be governed by what the scripture teaches (2 Timothy 3: 16-17; Psalms 19:7-14); Psalms 119:1-8, 103-105; 129-130). Our Conduct is to be governed.

3. **Walking in Gods Words: [3]** Ordering our steps=Listening to what God lays on our hearts - Listen to his promise
4. **Wisdom:** [4] Jesus is the personification of Wisdom. For the Christian, Gods Words, the Bible is our standard and guide.
5. **The Holy Spirit** [5](Begetter of Jesus Matt 1:18, 20; Luke 1:35)
6. **Response to negativity**/turn into a Godly act. Proper conduct is accepted, rewarded, while improper, unacceptable conduct is punished. (Psalms 1:6; John 5: 28-29; Romans 2:1-16; Galatians 6:7-8).
7. **Divine Ordering**: [6] The use of intelligence=God's leadership=Wisdom. God is accountable to no one because of His perfect character (Job 33:13).
8. **Answering the How Do You Do It? –question. [7] Moral principles written and unwritten, understood to be the norm in a culture.**
9. **Making some sense [8]** in the process, and in the world around us, as we strive to be productive/creating happiness. God's Word, the Bible, is our standard and guide. Our conduct is to be governed in everything by what the Scriptures teach.

(Discussion themes related to the Bible and God's teachings as they relate to our daily lives).

Course Description: Understanding Christian Ethics describes that a set of moral principles written or unwritten, generally are understood to be the norm in a culture. There must be a standard and guide for correct and good ethics, and for the Christian, God's Word, the Bible, is our standard and guide. Our conduct is to be governed in everything by what the Scriptures teach. (2 Timothy 3: 16-17; Psalms 119: 1-8, 103-105, 129-130). The Bible is the only infallible (incapable of error, trustworthy) rule of faith and practice.

Course Objectives: Understanding Christian Ethics is a study of beliefs or standards that include correct and good actions. Accountability is being required to account or answer for one's actions and conduct. The biblical concept means that people are answerable to certain human authorities, but, most importantly, to God (Romans 13: 1-2; 14:P12). Proper conduct is accepted, rewarded, while improper, unacceptable conduct is punished. (Psalms 1:6; John 5:28-29; Romans 2: 1-16; Galatians 6: 7-8). God is accountable to no one because of His perfect character (Job 33: 13).

Course Requirement: (Schedule: TBA / EDI Committee – See suggested Text Breakdown below)

Connie Williams   This Life: Through Grace Hope and Mercy

Class Procedures: Classes will include readings, lectures and discussion. Attendance will be taken.

> Understanding Christian Ethics provides contemporary ethical issues that are substantive enough for a teaching tool use yet functionally oriented toward the local church.

Text Breakdown: (Thirteen Chapters in the text- can be taught in three to four sessions or more if necessary).

1. Why Study Christian Ethics
2. Understanding the New Testament
3. Living to the Glory of God
4. Ethics of Decisions
5. The Church World
6. Politics and Christian Discipleships
7. Preparing for Disappointment
8. Economic Life
9. Who we are
10. Peace
11. Issues of Life and Death
12. Concerns in Contemporary Life
13. A Christians View

(Christian Ethics) According to the Bible, (God's Word, in the Bible) -Jesus Calls Us into God's

Redemption Story [1] (God Makes Good on the promises God gave to Abraham and David (Luke 1:32-33, 54-55, 68-73) Clues about Jesus: Faith and Hope of Israel (**The Old and New Testament**) **Too many people are saying I'm forsaken—the Lord says-I will never leave you.** [2] (Hebrew 13: V 5-6) ***GREEN*** **reference:**

    The story of the creation of ***GREEN***, a novel and a Christian writer: Connie Williams (as Emilee in the narrative) applies **Christian Ethics** to her everyday life.

    A New York Agent decided to promote my new book *GREEN*. They wrote a four page review of it, and said, "Two readers have read the book and we both think it is wonderful. There is nothing that needs to be done—it's perfect. Some of the literature read like poetry."

    As it turned out, after some weeks, they (the agency) decided they wanted to add illustrations. (**The World outside of Church**) They learned that I did not want other editors and writers' names credited in my book, and besides they wanted me to pay the agency for the changes they were suggesting. First of all, *GREEN* qualifies under a mainstream novel, (over 55 thousand words) adult classification under certain length etc. It's not a children's book.

    So, I suggested, "If changes are needed, I am capable of making any "technical changes" such as elaboration, word choice and weaving." (**Politics and

Christian Discipline) So the BIG NEW YORK AGENCY saw that I felt capable and willing to make the necessary changes, but they ironically had a change at heart; they determined, in an email, "We have decided not to take on any new projects!"

I knew God would never forsake me—never leave me. (**Living to God's Glory**) I intelligently transformed negativity into a Godly act. (**Ethics of Decision making**) [3] Divine Ordering from God manifestation=use of intelligence=God's leadership=Wisdom.

Wisdom (according to *ITTNT*) [4]: (**Reflection: Who we Are**) is rather abstract idea about the divine ordering of the cosmos and about how we must perceive that order to live intelligently=we walk in accordance with Wisdom. The New Testament writers do not stop with tradition about David and his heir. The Holy Spirit as the begetter of Jesus [5] (Matt 1:18, 20; Luke 1:35). Jesus is God's Son and, as heir of David, epitomizes how God provides leadership for God's people. (**Christian Discipline**) [2] This is the leadership of a servant, a redeemer who gives his life for the deliverance of his people, however. They look to Jewish traditions about "Wisdom" to talk about who Jesus is. Jesus is the personification of Wisdom connecting people to God as they walk in accordance with Wisdom. (Seen as female=she was created at the very beginning of God's creative activity (Prov 8:22) and worked alongside God in the creation of heaven and earth: Wisdom as "a pure emanation

(Peace) of the glory of the Almighty...a reflection of eternal light...an image of his goodness" (Wis 7:25-26), who enters human souls and "makes them friends of God" (**Issues of Life and Death**) (Wis 7:27).

Divine Ordering: [6] I indelibly knew that when I walk with God—he promised to never leave me=Jesus' faith and hope. But to know this, I had to order my steps in his words. (**Concerns of a Contemporary World**) Listen to his promise. He had already defeated the devil, so I didn't need to refight a battle that was already won. Well, I didn't fight with the New York Agent. When, in a phone call, from the agent, I was told "I've decided to not take on any new projects."

I simply responded, "Thank you for your response." I kept it simple, because I know my Lord. (**Christian Ethics**) So I got all prayed up and said. *GREEN* is about to come out! I went to work, sometimes from sun up to sun down. But He will not put more on us than we can bear. Two months later *GREEN* went to press under my own publication imprint AWAP. She (the book) was published February, 2015 and now available in: Barnes and Noble; Amazon Books; Walmart Supercenter; Book a Million; GoodReads.com; Get Textbooks.com; Charlotte Mecklenburg Public Library and Monroe-Union County Public Library; the James B. Duke Memorial Library, Johnson C. Smith, and available in seven different countries. He will never leave

Connie Williams   This Life: Through
                                   Grace Hope and Mercy

you=order your steps in his words. Thank you, Jesus for this favor.

Notes

DeSilver & Emerson B. Powery. ***Invitation to the New Testament***. Nashville, TN: Abingdon Press. 2005.

Lucado, Max. Imagine Your Life Without Fear. Thomas Nelson, Nashville: 2009. 978-0-8499-2020-2. [1]

Mark Nepo - spiritual writer, poet, philosopher, healing arts teacher ... *http://marknepo.com/*

Musselman, Reverend W.B. ***Bible Expositor and Illuminator****.* Ohio: A Union Gospel Press. 2008.

Tilliman, Jr, William M. ***Understanding Christian Ethics***. Fort Worth, TX: Broadman Press. 1988 (Syllabus: partly inspired by Portia Hammon, "The Missionary Training Instituted."). [2]

The Holy Bible: ***The New Testament***. Hebrew 13 V 15-16 (Rev. Dr. Lynch's teaching), Ebenezer Baptist Church. Charlotte, NC: 2014.

Willis, Avery T. Jr. and Kay Moore. ***The Disciple's Personality***. Nashville, TN: LifeWay Press. 2016

Williams, Connie. **Emily's Blues**. Charlotte, North Carolina: A Williams Acorn Publication. 2016. ISBN 978-0-692-63019-8

Williams, Connie. **Green**. Charlotte, North Carolina: A Williams Acorn Publication. 2015. ISBN 978-0-692-322371-7

Family ties

Left to right Rows: 1) Raven and friends, Pricilla, Dawn
2) Ishmael and great-grandson Mondi, Camilla, me and grandchildren. 3) Grandson Cory, Grandsons Jerry and Keith, Jerry Dean, and great-grandsons Josiah and Donavon; Granddaughter Rita and husband Mirthel.

Family ties

Left to right Rows: 1) My parents, my siblings and me
2) Great-grandchildren, the homestead in Monroe, Four of Daddy's brothers with Mama. 3) Our grandparents,
3) My grandparents on Daddy's side and siblings; my great-grands with their mom in TX; Rob and me.

Sources

Douglass, Frederick. "Oration, Delivered in Corinthian Hall, Rochester, July 5, 1852." Black Writers of America. Richard Barksdale and Kenneth Kinnamon. The Macmillan Company. New York: 1972.

Genesis 6: Life, Hope & Truth)

Haley, Alex. Letters to the author. Aug- Oct. 1989-1991.

http://articles.latimes.com/1992-02-12/news/vw-1608_1_alex-haley

https://brianchouston.com/2016/06/22/behold-i-do-

McManus, Cory, Senior Attorney at McManus Law Firm, Monroe, NC. The North Carolina General Assembly Statues: "Stalking and False Imprisonment." Consultation: Connie Williams. 6 Nov. 2017.

https://www.hymnal.net/en/hymn/h/694 *a-new-thing*

https://lifehopeandtruth.com/god/who-is-god/genesis-6/.

https://www.biblegateway.com/verse/en/Philippians%204%3A13

https://en.wikipedia.org/wiki/Lake_View_Terrace,_Los_Angeles

https://en.wikipedia.org/wiki/William_Marshall_(actor

http://scedc.caltech.edu/significant/borrego1968.html

http://www.desiringgod.org/articles/train-up-a-child-in-the-way-he-should-go

https://www.biblegateway.com/passage/?search Leviticus+1&version=NIV.

https://www.biblegateway.com/passage/?search=Ephesians+2%3A10&version=NLT

https://bible.org/seriespage/3-crossing-jordan-joshua-31-424

http://www.mims.com/indonesia/company/info/lapl

http://www.pewforum.org/2013/12/30/publics-views-on-human-evolution

https://en.wikipedia.org/wiki/Kuwait

https://www.cla.purdue.edu/from-plessy-to-brown/activities/2567750.pdf Jul 9, 2016 ...

https://en.wikipedia.org/wiki/Compton,_California

JobCorp:Program*https://recruiting.jobcorps.gov/Home/Information*

Scribner. "Literacy in Three Metaphors." Chicago Press: 1984.

"Soylent Green". www.youtube.com/?v=9IKVj415GU4

Toler, Stan and Alan Nelson. Baker Books. A division of Baker Publishing Group. Grand Rapids, Michigan: 2014

Urban Dictionary actually gives some helpful insight into the use of this word in this passage. The word that Paul uses was a Greek term called "**skubala**."

Williams, Connie. Pedagogies I and II first published in *John and Lale's Dance*. North Carolina: AWAP, 2016.

Williams, Connie. "Philosophy of Teaching." 2015: Unpublished.

Williams, Connie. Sermon: "My Story and Mission in Life." Ebenezer Baptist Church, Grier Memorial Chapel, Charlotte. 4 Apr. 1993.

Williams, Robert F. "Black Power," - Purdue College of Liberal Arts.

Emily Blues
A fictionalized autobiography based on a true story by Connie Williams

1989, Connie Williams gained recognition for her first novel, entitled **Emily's Blues**, a fictionalized autobiography is an excellent portrayal of a young girl in the 60s as she searched relentlessly for identity and a better life in an oppressive society. Her struggle to find dignity and self-worth should inspire girls around the globe to fight for the freedom and the respect they deserve. All females will find something relative to their lives in this emotional saga as Emily journeys from North Carolina, to New York, New Jersey, Washington, DC, and finally she makes an East to West odyssey in California to overcome. The story should serve as a wake-up call to males who are abusive to females or refuse to acknowledge their worth and importance. It should encourage fathers to become more involved in preparing their daughters for the pitfalls they might encounter in their relationships with males. **L. Hairston, Charlotte-Mecklenburg Schools**

While a teacher in the Union County School System, Williams founded The Emily's Blues Self-Actualization Project, a program designed to help deter school dropouts. Williams later penned "Emily's Dilemma," a stage play adaptation from her book that was performed at Livingstone College by her students, and received Honorable Mention by the Honorable Terry Sanford for an Arts Education Projects, supported by the Union County Community Arts Council in 1990. Emily's Blues was republished again in 2016. As a writer and educator, Williams wrote Emily's Blues to show young readers how she became "unstoppable" in overcoming an oppressed and impoverished background to get an education and become a professional educator. She received the Arts and Science Council Emerging Artist Award for Emily's Blues.

Emily's Blues is available at stores, online at Amazon

and on Amazon Kindle

Connie Williams

This Life: Through Grace Hope and Mercy

Green, a novel based on a true story by Connie Williams

1996, while a Writing Fellow at Headlands Center for the Arts, Sausalito, California, through an Award from the North Carolina Arts Council and the National Endowment for the Arts, Williams began writing her second novel **Green**, a story set in Monroe, North Carolina during the civil rights upheaval of the late 50s. Complicated, insightful, instructive and moving--with devastating guilt over the cause of a cornerstone family member's death-a precocious, eleven year old tri-racial girl, comes of age in Morris Town, a small city in North Carolina in the early 1960s. Emilee shows us her sensitive and very personal perception as she witnesses and learns of history via the refined extended family members during the South's Civil Rights Movement led by her cousin, the NAACP President, Robert F. Williams-"RW"--in Morris Town, North Carolina. As Emilee tries to understand her layered world of death, difficult relationships and her own identity, her world heaves with rebel flag waving Ku Klux Klansmen's deliberate racial violent upheaval as their motorcades ride right pass her window.

Frye Gaillard, author and winner of the Alabama Library Association Book of the Year Award says, "Good description, good imagery and deliberate repetition. **GREEN** is an intriguing story."

The late, **Minister John C. Williams, son of Robert F. Williams quotes,** "I believe the work will do great things for young audiences who otherwise would know nothing about the late Robert F. Williams, the Civil Rights Activists. The history is relevant and important today."

Available at stores, online at Amazon and six different countries.

Jon and Lale's Dance

Williams' third novel Jon and Lale's Dance is the story that she was compelled to write. It is the story of her parents who were married for 68 years before their passing in 2010 and 2011 within four months of each other around the time of their birthdays.

Sixty plus years of marriage have gone by, and the couple, Jon and Lale, find themselves still totally devoted to each other, yet they cannot resist the daily temptations, from time to time, to slip back into their old habits of agitating each other at the most inopportune moments. Lale can't manage to leave the house to grocery shop for necessities with her daughter, Topia, for Jon's Doctor Pepper and jar of Jiffy peanut butter, without first "directing some insults" toward him about his need to "sit, do nothing and nap" at the kitchen table. And Jon cannot manage to resist using his quick-wit of accusations that stops Lale in her tracks each time she makes an attempt to prepare to leave the house, to get into the car with her daughter, Topia. And this is how their battles usually begin, that sometimes last all afternoon, until Jon wants to nap again. They each enjoy satirizing. Williams threads this story with humor, suspense, tragedy and the true-to-life sensitive facts about health issues such as dementia, crippling rheumatoid arthritis and cancer that so many families and senior citizens face, that may lead to their sometimes early demise in today's society

Confession of the Onion Ring King: A children's story for all ages, 2019.

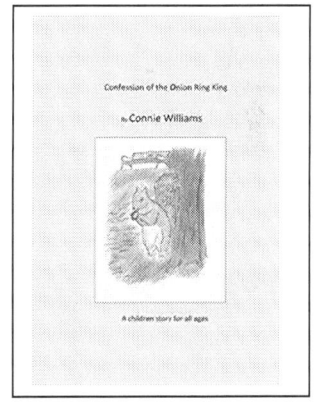

This is Williams first children's book that tells the story of a mischievous squirrel when he gets into trouble in the human world.

Also available at bookstores and online at Amazon.

About the Author

Connie Williams is a local figure known for her distinguished career as a skillful writer of prose and poetry. Until her retirement in 2014 she was an instructor of English Composition and Rhetoric at UNC, at Charlotte; a high school English instructor at Charlotte-Mecklenburg Schools and Union County Schools. Her inspirational, fictionalized autobiography, **Emily's Blues,** tells how a young divorcee and mother of four, went from poverty to a professional and was showcased in the "Dare to Dream Project", Z Smith Reynolds Foundation, 1990. She is the recipient of the Arts and Science Council Emerging Artist Award for her book. Her novel's stage play adaptation, entitled "Emily's Dilemma," received the Honorable Terry Sanford Award for Creativity Honorable Mention, and was performed at Livingstone College at Salisbury by her students.

Her dedication to arts education and outreach led Williams to create, the Emily's Blues Self-Actualization Project, and she volunteered her services to help deter high school dropouts. The program received the Union County Community Arts Council Grant for eight years at Piedmont High School where her book was used with students. She has volunteered her services to Healthy Mothers and Healthy Babies, the University of South Carolina, at Lancaster; International Young Writers Program, in Charlotte. She has presented readings and facilitated writing workshops at: Barnes and Noble, the Charlotte Public Library, Imagine On, Ebenezer Baptist Church, the Nile Theater, and UNC, Center City Campus at Charlotte; Spirit Square, Charlotte; Afro American Cultural Center, Charlotte. She is a Christa McAuliffe Fellow finalist.

She is a contributing author to the following publications: "Mama Allie's Talking Dogs..." stories and recipes of Carolina cuisine, **Hungry for Home,** Rogers. Novello Festival Press: 2003. A short story excerpt, **Emily's Blues**, and a collection of poetry, **The National Literary Circular**: 1990. Original poetry, **A**

Sun-filled Dream: 1989. Classroom consultant: ***A History of the World*** textbook: Houghton Mifflin: Boston. 1988. Williams is the recipient of the 1996 North Carolina Arts Council Award and The National Endowment for the Arts for a Fellowship at Headlands Center for the Arts, Sausalito, California, as an eight weeks artist- collaborator. She is a former Writing Fellow of the University of North Carolina, Charlotte, 1992. A native of Monroe, North Carolina, she has eleven siblings. Her parents celebrated their 68th wedding anniversary 2009 and passed shortly afterward in 2010 and 2011 within only four months of each other.

In 2015 Williams started her own publication company AWAP (A Williams' Acorn Publication) and published her first four books under her imprint.

Williams is a wife, mother, grand and great-grandmother. She graduated from Cal State University, Northridge (B.A. Degree), and the University of North Carolina, at Charlotte (M.Ed. Degree). She resides with her husband in North Carolina.

Made in the USA
Lexington, KY
14 November 2019